Mina A. Girgis

GALATIANS FOR TEENS

by

Mina A. Girgis

ST SHENOUDA'S MONASTERY
SYDNEY, AUSTRALIA
2024

Galatian for Teens

COPYRIGHT © 2024
St Shenouda Press

All rights reserved. Except for brief quotations in critical publications or reviews, no part of this book may be reproduced in any manner without prior written permission from the publisher.

ST SHENOUDA PRESS
8419 Putty Rd,
Putty, NSW, 2330

www.stshenoudapress.com

ISBN 13: 978-1-7635450-8-3

All scripture quotations, unless otherwise indicated, are taken from the New King James Version®. Copyright © 1982 by Thomas Nelson, Inc. Used by permission. All rights reserved.

About the Author:

Mina A. Girgis is a Youth and Sunday School servant at Archangel Michael and St Bishoy Coptic Orthodox Church, Mt Druitt, NSW. He is a High School English teacher and has a passion for reading and writing.

Cover Design:
Mariana Hanna
In and Out Creation Pty Ltd
www.inandoutcreations.com.au

Layout Design:
Hani Ghaly,
Begoury Graphics
begourygraphics@gmail.com

Contents

Chapter One	11
Chapter Two	21
Chapter Three	29
Chapter Four	37
Chapter Five	45
Chapter Six	53
Chapter Seven	59
Chapter Eight	65
Chapter Nine	73
Chapter Ten	79
Chapter Eleven	87
Chapter Twelve	93
Chapter Thirteen	101
Chapter Fourteen	107
Chapter Fifteen	113
Chapter Sixteen	119
Chapter seventeen	125
Chapter eighteen	131
Chapter nineteen	137
Chapter twenty	143

A Map of Galatia

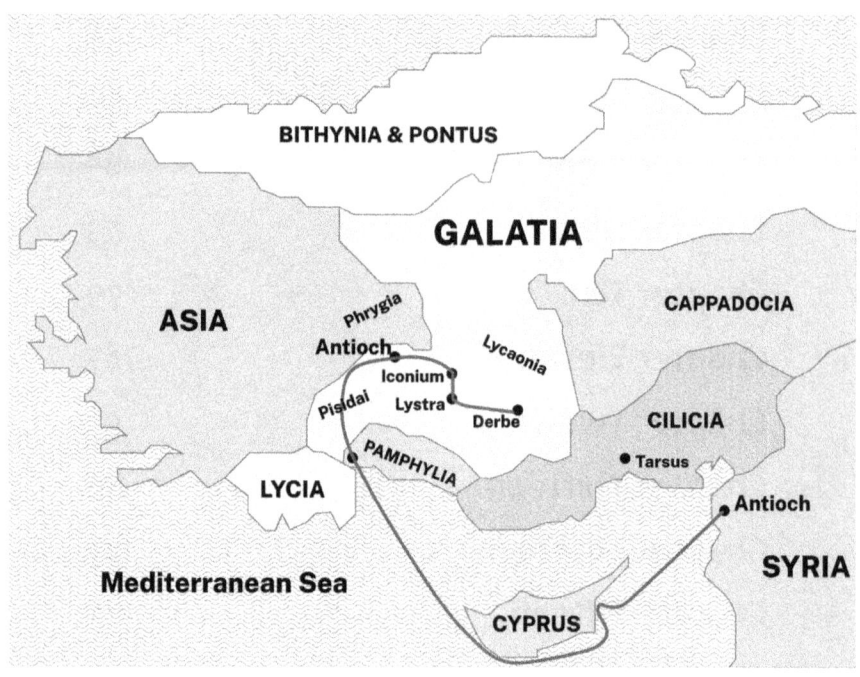

INTRODUCTION

The book of Galatians is an epistle directed to the church at Galatia (somewhere around modern-day Turkey). Galatia being a gentile church, was not necessarily aware of the Jewish practices of the Old Covenant. However, the church began to experience an influx of Christian Jewish preachers (referred to as Judaizers) explaining to them that although they were Gentile Christians, they must still partake in the laws of the Jewish Old Covenant. This emphasis on Jewish law is the central dispute throughout the letter, however, as is common in the letters of St. Paul, the book of Gentiles is filled with wisdom and teachings that are relevant to us all today.

In his letter to the Galatians, Paul cleverly structures his argument against adherence to the old law, in a very logical manner. He begins by first explaining his spiritual journey and "qualifications" that make him a worthy responder to the issue at hand. This first section can be seen as Paul's defence of his apostolic authority on the matter.

The second section speaks about the concept of the Holy Spirit and how the Holy Spirit is a gift to the church. Paul explains the impact of the Holy Spirit on both churches and Christians and the constant need to battle against the flesh to remain steadfast in the faith. He uses this argument to explain that through the cross of Christ, there is no longer a need to adhere to the ways of the Old Covenant.

What makes Galatians relevant to us today is Paul using the Galatian dispute to re-administer the Gospel of Christ to them while emphasising the importance of never changing nor subtracting from the words of the Gospel. He also invites the readers to reorient their thinking to focus on salvation always and to understand that salvation is through Christ and that through

Christ we are all one. In this epistle, we also see the very famous fruits of the spirit, as Paul explains how we can avoid serving the flesh and serve the spirit instead.

Character Profile – St Paul the Apostle

St Paul was considered by many to be one of the main driving forces behind the mass movement of Christianity within the first century. A large portion of the New Testament is filled with the epistles of Paul and the story of his life as a preacher. Paul, however, was not always Christian and originally used his Hebrew name, Saul. Saul was born in Tarsus, South Turkey, to a family of extremely devout Jews. Although he is ethnically Jewish, Saul was a citizen of the Roman Empire as Turkey, at the time, was a Roman province. Saul grew up as an extremely zealous Jew who was well versed in the scriptures and was a member of the Sanhedrin. In addition to Saul's Jewish knowledge and authority, he was also well educated in Greek and Greek philosophy. To put it simply, Saul was an extremely prominent figure and leading authority for the Jews.

His early life as a member of the Sanhedrin, saw him persecuting Christians with incessant fervour. Saul hated Christians with a passion, particularly the Christian idea that the Messiah was killed in the manner of a criminal and among criminals. Hence, Saul made it his goal to eradicate Christianity, and he was effective at his role. As seen in the book of Acts, Saul assured the death of Stephen the first martyr by stoning. Saul's devoutness to the Jewish faith made him believe that he was doing the right thing by killing Christians. Everything changed for Saul, however, on the road to Damascus.

Saul was on his way to Damascus for the purpose of apprehending and killing the Christians in Damascus. As often was the case in Saul's life, God had a different plan for him. On the road to Damascus, he was blinded, by a piercing light coming from the sky. As he lay on the floor dazed and in shock, he heard Christ's voice asking, "Saul, Saul, why are you persecuting me?" when Saul asked who was speaking to him, the voice replied saying, "I am Jesus, whom you are persecuting."

From then on, everything changed for Saul. Saul thus became a Christian, and with the same zealousness that he persecuted and denounced Christianity, he went on to preach it. To put this in context, imagine the most infamous, Christian killing terrorist in the world. Now imagine that all of a sudden, he has an epiphany and becomes one of the greatest Christian evangelists in the world.

Contrary to popular belief, God did not change Saul's name to Paul as a sign of him becoming Christian. Paul was always his Greek name, and as he began to preach Christianity to gentiles, he decided to use his Greek name.

St. Paul's impact on Christianity speaks for itself. Many consider Paul to be the greatest figure in Christian history, right after Jesus Christ. Fourteen of the twenty-seven books of the New Testament were written by Paul, with half of the book of Acts being attributed to the stories of his mission.

Since Paul was a renowned and infamous persecutor of Christians, his preaching was effective as he was able to show the power of Christ through his conversion. Many people turned to Christianity through Paul in which he remained in contact with through his letters. Through his letters, we can see how passionate, God-fearing, loving, clever and committed Paul was to God and his mission.

Paul was not exempt from working, though. When he wasn't preaching, he spent his time working on his trade which was tent-making. This job was his primary and only source of income when he was not relying on charity from fellow believers.

Eventually, Paul, as a result of his preaching, was confined to a jail cell until his demise by capital punishment in Rome. Once again, God subverted Paul's plans and replaced them with His own. Paul always dreamed of preaching to the great city of Rome and made that his final goal. However, he was instead imprisoned in Rome and killed there. One might assume that his imprisonment severely negated his ability to preach the Gospel, but since all things are possible with God, Paul's most significant impact to Christianity occurred while he was imprisoned.

Paul confirms this in the following verse: "Now I want you to know, brothers and sisters, that what has happened to me has actually served to advance the Gospel. As a result, it has become clear throughout the whole palace guard and to everyone else that I am in chains for Christ. And because of my chains, most of the brothers and sisters have become confident in the Lord and dare all the more to proclaim the Gospel without fear." (Phillipains 1:12-18)

Chapter One

Pauls Authority as an Apostle

The beginning of the epistle to the Galatians is opened passionately and immediately to a counterargument from Paul. Paul starts by saying,

"Paul, an apostle (not from men nor through man, but through Jesus Christ and God the Father who raised Him from the dead.)"

As you can see, Paul's introduction of himself is written specifically to make it clear to the readers that his Apostleship was not chosen by a man nor given to him through a man, but he was specifically chosen by God. As you know, Paul is clearly referring to his divine revelation on the road to Damascus as it was God who stopped him and guided him to the path of Christianity, declaring him as an apostle. But why does Paul begin his letter like this? Well, this is a direct response to the Judaizers in the church of Galatia who were using the argument and notion that since Paul was not a one of the twelve Apostles, he does not have any authority over the churches and cannot demand that they do not abide by Jewish law. This was a common argument against Paul at the time, and so Paul sets the record straight and makes it clear that he IS an apostle, and he was in fact chosen by God just like the disciples.

Who are the Judaizers?

Before we can continue, understanding exactly who the Judaizers were, is extremely important. To understand the Judaizers, we need to understand Jewish Law. The law that the Jew's adhered to is what we read in the first five books of the Bible, referred to by the Jews as the Torah. Throughout these books there are specific explanations and rules given to the Jews from God on how to live, how to take care of yourselves, how to act and of course, when not to work (Sabbath). These laws were in addition to the ten commandments and were more practically oriented than spiritually. Of course, this law was extremely important before the coming of the Messiah. God used these laws to separate the Jewish people from the gentiles and confirm them as God's chosen people. God needed to make sure that they were healthy, God driven, and unique so that they could one day bring forth the Messiah who would then become the saviour of the world.

However, in Christ's own words, "Do not think that I came to destroy the Law or the Prophets. I did not come to destroy but to fulfill." The coming of Christ is the fulfillment of the law, meaning that the law was put in place to pave the way for Christ. Now, back to the Judaizers, they were Jewish Christians who believed that Christ was the messiah, however, they believed that Christians still needed to observe the old Jewish laws that Christ stated that He had fulfilled. They believed that salvation came from believing in Christ and adhering to the Jewish Law. Thus, they preached this throughout the churches scattered across the early church and even to the Gentiles, since they were aware that their teachings did not align with the teachings of St. Paul, they condemned Paul, exclaiming that he was not a true apostle and was not chosen by God. As we now continue throughout the book of Galatians, you will

> **What the Fathers Say**
>
> "If you believe what you like in the Gospel, and reject what you don't like, it is not the Gospel you believe, but yourself."
>
> – St. Augustine

> **What the Fathers Say**
>
> They wish, to disturb the gospel of Christ but cannot prevail, because it is of such a nature that it cannot be other than the truth.
> – St. Jerome

see Paul's passionate arguments against the Judaizers and the evidence behind his own Apostolic authority.

Paul vs the Judaizers

As Paul continues to verse three, he quickly reiterates the gospel, integrating it within his greeting. This can be seen as a method of grounding the foundation of his letter with the gospel of Christ. Paul then marvels at the churches within Galatia as they have so quickly turned from the Gospel to a different gospel. Paul stating that what they believe is a different gospel is an extremely weighted claim. He elaborates on what he means saying, "Which is not another; but there are some who trouble you and want to pervert the gospel of Christ." Paul makes it clear that he is not saying that they have chosen another gospel entirely, but a perversion of the current one. It is then reiterated by Paul, the dangers of changing or preaching another gospel, calling those who do this, "Accursed."

This warning is very relevant to us today, the global accessibility of the Bible means that anyone can pick up the bible and interpret things whichever way they want and take verses out of context. It is extremely important for all of us today to be vigilant in the way we receive the words of the bible and the way we quote the words of the Bible. Sometimes we can even use verses out of context for our own benefit, but this is not correct. The Bible must be seen as a whole and grounded in the tradition of the Fathers that has been given to us.

Chapter One

This idea leads us to Pauls following point. Paul makes it clear to the church of Galatia that he does not write these letters or preach the gospel in order to please men or persuade men, but whatever he does it is for Christ as he is a bondservant of Christ. Paul is thus teaching us what service looks like, when we serve, we must emphasise to ourselves that our service is not for glory nor the pleasing of men or the persuading of men. We are serving for Christ and Christ only that he may work through us and that we may be like Him as he also served other during His time on earth.

"For I neither received it from man, nor was I taught it, but it came through the revelation of Jesus Christ"

Once again, Paul reiterates that the gospel he received was not from man but from Christ. However, this time Paul backs up this idea by talking about his past. He begins to go through his history as a persecutor of Christians during his time as a Jew, emphasising that he not only persecuted the church but aimed to destroy it. This notion is extremely important to be aware of when reading the letters of St. Paul. Paul was not simply a persecutor of Christians but wanted to completely eradicate Christianity and Paul's effectiveness in his goal actually led to the fleeing of many Christians to Damascus. The notoriety of Paul's Christian persecution is also emphasised in the book of Acts when God tells Ananias to go meet with Paul, Ananias responds with fear and animosity saying,

"Lord, I have heard from many about this man, how much harm he has done to Your

> **What the Fathers Say**
>
> We should accept whatever happens in this life, even though it seems difficult to bear, because we know that it is for our salvation and God never sends us anything beyond our strength to endure.
>
> – St. Basil the Great

What the Fathers Say

When the spirit is not distracted by external things or preoccupied with study, then it returns to itself; and by itself it ascends to the thought of God.
– St. Anthony the Great

saints in Jerusalem. And here he has authority from the chief priests to bind all who call on your name." (Acts 9:13-14) When reading this passage, remember that Ananias would have most likely been a target for Paul's persecution, furthermore emphasising God's grace and ability to transform bad to good.

Paul's story, thus, is a testament to God's will and how He can work through people. Our God is a God that is so great that he takes all that is bad and makes it good. God saw Paul's passion and zeal in persecuting Christians and knew that Paul's same passion and zeal could be used for the furtherance of the gospel and thus, God made it so. This is what Paul is emphasising here, he is making it clear that his authority and apostleship must come from Christ as how else could the most notorious persecutor of Christians suddenly change his ways?

Another point we can take from this is that Christ does not look at our past and

People, Places &Things

The Jewish Roots of Christianity

Early Christian was begun and spread by Jews. As a result, when Christianity was spread to the Jews, it was difficult for them to comprehend that salvation was now for all and that they no longer needed to practise their Biblical cultural laws. Since the Jews associated much of their identity with the law and their culture, it would take time for them to understand that Christianity is no longer Judaism and the Law has been fulfilled. Hence, the Judaizers who loved their cultural practices attempted to claim that those practices were needed for salvation.

Chapter One

former conduct when he chooses us for service, nor does He care about our prior sins once we decide to repent. Do not think that your past can ever stop you from serving God or serving within the church!

> *"But when it pleased God, who separated me from my mother's womb and called me through His grace, to reveal His Son in me, that I might preach Him among the Gentiles, I did not immediately confer with flesh and blood, nor did I go up to Jerusalem to those who were apostles before me; but I went to Arabia and returned again to Damascus. Then after three years I went up to Jerusalem to see Peter."*

The above three verses begin to reveal to us the unique and crucial importance of this epistle as it gives us insight into the life of St. Paul that cannot be find elsewhere. Upon your first reading of the said verses, you might find yourself asking "Why is Paul saying this?" "What importance does it have?" "Why is he telling us he went to Arabia?" Once again, Paul is making clear his argument for his Apostolic authority. What you might not have known, is that these verses link to Paul's argument in which he claims that he did not receive the gospel from a man but from Christ himself. Church tradition teaches us that during St. Paul's sojourn in Arabia, Christ revealed to him the gospel. His time in Arabia can be seen as a Pre-service retreat, in which St. Paul took time to reflect on the sudden change in his life and pray to God for wisdom and understanding. This sojourn is an important lesson to all of us.

Before beginning a service, it is customary withing the Coptic Church to partake in retreat. Christ, before beginning his ministry,

---

What the Fathers Say

Those who are taught by men, when they have been vehement and hot in the opposite cause, require time and much ingenuity for their conversion. But he who was so suddenly converted and was rendered clean and sober at the very peak of his madness had obviously received a divine vision and teaching
– St. John Chrysostom

spent forty days in the wilderness, fasting and praying. It is for this reason, that priests, on the day of their ordination leave society and spend forty days in the monastery. It is, of course, also befitting that Paul should also retreat from the world before beginning his ministry and in doing so, just like Christ, Paul teaches us a valuable lesson.

When we serve as Christians, we hope and pray that God may work through us for the furtherance of his Gospel. This is a big responsibility and to serve God's children cannot be taken light heartedly. In order to fully accept and undertake this responsibility, we as Christians must do like Christ and His apostles and retreat from distractions and pray and fast. It is expected that during this period we get closer to God and receive the wisdom that aids us in service. However, it is not only before service that we should retreat and pray. When life gets tough or when we

Christian Retreat

Retreating from the world and having quiet time is important for all members of the church, not just priests and monks. Just like Paul, the Coptic church encourages that all servants of the church engage in quiet time and spiritual retreats before beginning any service. A retreat away from worldly matters helps us reorient our thinking towards God and strengthens our relationship with him before we go on to serve.

People, Places &Things

have a tough decision to make, retreat. Remember that in stillness you will hear God's voice. So, in practise, teach yourself to retreat and resort to God the instant you are met with hardship or have a difficult decision to make. When St. Paul's entire life was flipped upside down and his entire sense of being was turned by God's grace, Paul retreated and sought-after God and look at the fruits that St. Paul continues to bear today.

REFLECTION

When was the last time you had quiet time? When was the last time you freed up some time in your day and said I will just sit with God and talk to him and listen in the silence and peace of his presence. Let's try our best to make some time today to actually sit with God in silence and engage in our own retreat into our souls and speak to God.

Chapter Two

As we reach the end of Chapter One of Galatians, Paul begins to conclude his argument concerning his right to apostleship. What is interesting among these final verses is that we see Paul place emphasis on the fact that he did not see any apostle except for Peter and James. The reason he pushed for the Galatians to know this is to show them that he was not regularly amongst the disciples of Christ and did not receive the gospel from them, instead he only saw a select couple of the disciples. This section once again counters any arguments from the Judaizers against Paul. Since the Judaizers looked at Paul as someone who was not an apostle, as according to their standard, an apostle of Christ needed to have seen Christ and seen the gospel preached to them by Christ. Summarising Paul's argument from his point of view, Paul explains the following:

1. I was a notorious persecutor that was known to all Christians

2. I was a well-learned and passionate Jew with a great understanding of the Old Testament

3. When you consider that last two points, there is no way I could have been converted to Christianity by man

4. I did not even meet many apostles after my revelation on the road to Damascus, meaning men did not teach me the Gospel

5. Hence, I must have received the Gospel from Christ and His Divine Providence

As you can see, Paul's argument is structured highly intelligently and covers all bases against the Judaizers.

Finally, Paul concludes stating that those who did not know him as a Christian, glorified God when they met him. This was because they only knew Paul as a man who tried to destroy the church but now, he preaches for the church. Once again, we see the glorious mercy of God and how He takes what is bad within us and turns it good.

> Paul addresses Jewish Culture and conflict between apostles

Now as we venture into the second chapter of Galatians, Paul begins to specifically address circumcision. Before he addresses circumcision, however, he makes it clear to readers that upon his return to the disciples after fourteen years, Paul makes it clear that he expressed the gospel to them that he preached to the gentiles to make sure that he was not teaching the wrong thing. These introductory lines prove to us that gospel Paul received through revelation and then preached to the gospels does not contradict the gospels of the apostles, concluding Paul's argument against the Judaizers.

St. Paul then addresses the controversial topic of circumcision. We know that circumcision was the covenant given to Abraham and all Jewish as a sign of God's promise to them. However, since Christ arrived on Earth and granted salvation to all peoples, the need for circumcision was obviously abolished. Unfortunately, this did not sit well with certain Jewish Christians as they were very passionate about their

What the Fathers Say

"According to thy mercy, pour out upon me, who am miserable, at least one small drop of grace to make me understand and be converted, that I might make at least some small effort to correct myself."

– St. Ephrem the Syrian

> **What the Fathers Say**
>
> For neither the Lord nor His holy apostles have left us the least doubt about these things; but in the most plain language they have pronounced there is one faith only, and that this alone is true, divine, and saving.
> – St. Athanasius

traditions and held onto them with zeal. Thus, Paul explains that there is no need for circumcision and uses Titus as an example (a Greek missionary and apostle of St. Paul) of a gentile who knew that he did not need to be circumcised. Paul explains that the only reason this "false doctrine" of gentiles needing to be circumcised came into the church was through the stealthy teaching of Judaizers who sought to bring the church back into "bondage" by returning her to Jewish customs and cultures. Paul states that he and the apostles did not submit to these teachings for a single moment so that the true gospel may continue to be spread, Paul is emphasising once again that the incessance of Jewish culture within Christianity is not an aspect of the gospel.

This is important to consider in our own lives. We should be weary to understand the differences between our culture and our faith and never combine the two.

Paul's Persuasive Skills

History has taught as that St. Paul knew, Greek, Aramaic, Hebrew and potentially Latin and thus was obviously highly educated. Something that he does not get enough credit for, however, is his ability to persuade. Paul was actually a master rhetoric! Rhetoric refers to the art of effective and persuasive speaking and writing. As you can see from the way he plans out his arguments above, he was obviously very logical and persuasive in his methods. See how he naturally follows a logical flow of persuasion just like you would like in an essay-writing class. This further shows us how God picked the perfect man for the job and used his talents for the good of the Gospel.

People, Places &Things

Continuing, Paul explains that he was tasked to preach the gospel to the uncircumcised (Gentiles) and Peter was tasked to preach the Gospel to the circumcised (Jews). This decision was made with wisdom as the apostles that tasked Paul to preach to the Gentiles, understood that he had a Roman citizenship, meaning that he could travel freely around the Roman empire; and that he was highly educated, meaning that he could deal with highly philosophic communities such as the Greeks (as we see in Acts 17 in which Paul preaches to Greeks in Athens and quotes Greek philosophers in his sermon). Paul mentions that the disciples James, Peter and John (considered as pillars of the gospel) gave him the right hand of fellowship to preach. What exactly does the "right hand of fellowship" mean, however. St Augustine, explains saying that the right hand of fellowship is "the sign of harmony, the sign of agreement, that what they had learnt from him differed in no respect from them."

Once again, Paul made sure to mention this so that he could explain to the Judaizers that he was in fact chosen specifically to preach to the Gentiles for a reason and that the gospel that he received from Christ through revelation is no different than the gospel of the Pillars (James, Peter and John).

Using Paul as an example, remember that we are called in our lives to be witnesses to Christ and to preach his Gospel. Paul as a Roman citizen used his Roman citizenship and education to spread the Gospel, so we to must use our talents and the means that are available to us top spread the good news of Christianity to all. This can be done by finding a way to glorify God in all that you do, and if you're doing that correctly, than people might see God through you without you having to utter a single word.

An example of this can be during school, imagine you're really good at art, and when art class comes around and your teacher tells you to draw something or someone you love, you might be compelled to draw a picture of Jesus. Other students might look at that and begin to ask, "Why does this person love Jesus so much?" or "Why would they use their drawing talent to draw a religious figure?" in a situation such as that you are effectively preaching without saying anything. Maybe those other students can one day will come to you and ask why you love Jesus, and in that moment, you can spread the Gospel.

Simple acts such as these spread the story of salvation without having to preach outwardly! So, use your talents and what you have wisely! And remember that if you're glorifying God in all that you do, then you're preaching without preaching without opening your mouth.

As each one has received a gift, minister it to one another, as good stewards of the manifold grace of God (I Peter 4:10)

REFLECTION

At the end of the day I sometimes like to reflect on the events of my day and consider what moments I thought of God or maybe even glorified God. When I do this, it's puts into perspective how often I forget about God in my day to day life. Ask yourself, what have you done to remember God today? What have you do to glorify God today? Let's make it a habit of making sure we glorify God every single day and in everything that we do.

Chapter Three

CHAPTER THREE

Dispute Between Paul and Peter

Now at 2:11 we see an integral part of the Epistle to the Galatians; we see Paul rebuke Peter and "Withstand him to his face" correcting him and blaming him for misdirection among the Jews and Gentiles. Upon reading this the first time you might be a bit confused and think "How can Paul lecture Peter and highlight his errors like that? Are they both not Apostles? Or why would Paul mention this in his Epistle, is he trying to embarrass Peter?" Of course, this was not St. Pauls intent. As Paul always says, his intention and goals are entirely for the furtherance of the gospel. Paul's issues with Peter's behaviours here was the fact that Peter was allowing himself to be stuck between two ideologies. When the Judaizers were around, Peter would not eat with Gentiles (Jewish law requests that Jews do not eat with Gentiles as they have their own dietary customs), but when the Judaizers were not around Peter would gladly eat with the Gentiles. Paul's role in this situation is not to puff himself above Peter, and he is not mentioning the situation to embarrass Peter of put him down. Paul is explaining that, even to Peter, an esteemed disciple of Christ, he made his beliefs known to him and encouraged his consistency. Peter being a human being that makes mistakes like all of us, made a mistake concerning Jewish law and Paul simply nudged him back onto the right path. Paul explicitly says to Peter:

"If you, being a Jew, live in the manner of Gentiles and not as the Jews, why do you compel Gentiles to live as Jews?"

Paul is explaining his concerns with Peter, showing to him the error of his ways. Explaining to Peter and all of us that you cannot preach something that you yourself do not follow. We know from Acts Chapter 10, that Peter had a vision in which God spoke to him saying that he could now eat from the unclean animals, thus telling us that Peter was in fact living like a Gentile. In addition to this, Paul elaborates and explains to us that we are justified by our faith in Jesus Christ, justification in this context refers to our salvation and completion of our Christian life which is to be with Christ. However, this does not mean that we are saved simply because we believe and have faith that Jesus Christ is real and Christianity is the truth. Of course, that would be completely unfair. Instead, what Paul is trying to explain to us, is that our salvation comes from our faith in Jesus Christ and our faith in Jesus Christ pushes us to act

> **What the Fathers Say**
>
> The Jews abstain from certain animals because they are commanded to do so by the Law. But the Christian Church does not observe these restrictions because they were symbols and figures of what was to come.
> – St. John Chrysostom

Paul's Disagreements

Paul also had another disagreement with another apostle, not only Peter. In Acts 15:36 Paul disagreed with Barnabas over allowing Mark to join them in their journey. To summarise, Paul's point was that Mark was not yet ready as he had abandoned them at another time but Barnabas insisted that Mark should join them. Because of their disagreement, both parties went their separate ways. Now we can look at that and think, "How can these apostles argue like that?" Or understand that they were human and had disagreements but that didn't take away from their love for each other. God also took that situation and allowed good to come out from it as Mark went out to preach in Alexandria and write one of the four gospels.

> **What the Fathers Say**
>
> Correct your brother, not as a foe, nor as an adversary exacting a penalty, but as a physician providing medicine
> – St. John Chrysostom

like-Christ. He emphasises that the works of the law do not save. This was entirely evident through the pharisees whom Christ constantly condemned. The problem with the pharisees was that they were so strict on the rules of the law and followed them rigidly, yet inside their deeds were bad and they were not good people. This notion is what Christ is referring when he says these words in Matthew 23:

> *Woe to you, scribes and Pharisees, hypocrites! For you cleanse the outside of the cup and dish, but inside they are full of extortion and self-indulgence." (Matthew 23:25)*

Now a way to relate this to us as modern-day Christians is through the sacraments. Unlike the Old Testament laws, the sacraments are very important to our salvation today. However! Simply partaking of the sacraments does not guarantee our salvation. Just like the pharisees, we can be having communion, going to church, baptised, and regularly having confession and yet the inside of our cup is dirty. The sacraments that we partake in are tools for salvation that do not guarantee salvation. On the other hand, we cannot have faith in Christ and be a good Christian without partaking in the sacraments. Christ has always said that you must be baptised through water and spirit; you must partake of my body and blood; you must repent your sins. We need to view the sacraments and our personal faith and deeds as two things that can never be separated.

The reason for the strict dietary laws for Jews begins in Exodus. After God took the Israelites outside of Egypt, he established laws for the nation of Israel on top of the Ten Commandments that Moses received on

Chapter Three

Mount Sinai. An example of this can be seen in Exodus 23:19, in which God tells the Israelites that they can only eat animals with cloven hooves that eat grass, and that the practice of eating shellfish is not allowed. There are many more dietary rules that we wont go through but to put it simply, the Jews had a strict diet. Today that diet is called the "Kosher" diet. Now, reading all these rules in Exodus, you'll definitely find yourself asking, "What exactly is the need for all these dietary laws, and why did God backtrack in the New Testament and tell Peter to eat of any animal he wanted?"

Well, a good way to look at the dietary laws present in Exodus is to understand God's goal for the Jewish people. The Jews were God's chosen people not because they were better than everyone else or because God loved them more, but because they were charged with bringing forth the messiah who will grant salvation to us all. So obviously, a responsibility such as that comes with a lot of discipline. In the wise words of Uncle Ben, "with great power, comes great responsibility." This meant that the Jews had to stand out, they couldn't look like the nations around them, they couldn't eat the same foods as they needed to be healthy, and they could not concern themselves too deeply with gentiles as well as they needed to have their own unique rituals and customs. These laws served a functional purpose, such as health obviously they needed to be healthy in order to live long enough so Christ could arrive, and also these laws meant that to the rest of the world they were unique and stood out, a beacon of salvation until salvation itself arrived in the form of Jesus Christ. In the case of Peter, once Christ had arrived and granted

> **What the Fathers Say**
>
> *In the matter of correction, the precept of the Lord must be observed: not to reproach a neighbour in the presence of others but to take him aside and reprove him privately*
> – St. Basil the Great

salvation to the whole world, these laws have now been fulfilled they have served their purpose. Peter's vision commanded him that he could now eat anything he wanted which also symbolised preaching to the gentiles.

"Do not think that I came to destroy the Law or the Prophets. I did not come to destroy but to fulfill." (Matthew 5:17-20)

To summarise the chapter, the dispute between Peter and Paul teaches us too main things. Beginning with, no one in perfect. This is entirely evident throughout both the Old Testament and New Testament. It is very common to see apostles and prophets struggle with their sins throughout the Bible and this is great for us to look at and learn from their mistakes. In addition to that, their experiences teach us not to despair in regard to our own sin as everyone has their own struggles. Specifically, the situation between Peter and Paul teaches us that it is okay to speak to your friends if you think they are going down a wrong path or are doing something that you think is troubling. I'm sure we have all been involved in an experience where we have a friend or a family member who is partaking in a certain sin or going down the wrong path. We might think to ourselves in that situation, "Oh, it's best I don't speak to him/her so it does not look like I'm judging him/her" or that it might cause drama between you and that other person. Christ tells us exactly what to do in that situation:

"If your brother sins against you, go and tell him his fault, between you and him alone." (Matthew 18:15)

However, it is important to note that if we are willing to make known to our friends and companions their faults, we too should also be willing to hear their instruction to us likewise. King Solomon speaks of this saying,

"He who keeps instruction is in the way of life, But he who refuses correction goes astray" (Proverbs 10:17)

However, when giving advice or correcting a person, it is important to note that this must be done with wisdom. If a friend's sin is impacting you or others around them then in that case it would be wise for you to take them aside and let them know, as Christ said. However, if it is a sin that only concerns him or herself, then it is best to leave that to their confession father unless this person explicitly asks you for advice. Looking back, once again, at the situation between Paul and Peter, it seemed that Peter's way was impacting the church congregation and adding fuel to the contention between gentiles and Judaizers. Which is why Paul was so outward in his confrontation and why he decided to include it in his epistle.

It is important to reflect on situations in which we feel that maybe we should speak up to a friend, but not only that but to also reflect on our friendships and our friendship cultures. Do we have a culture with our friends that invites advice and correction?

Do I feel comfortable receiving correction from my friends?

Am I comfortable to speak up to my friend to tell them something that they might not like to hear?

Remember, that friends are a blessing from God and who you surround yourself outwardly impacts you. Remember that Paul says,

> "Do not be deceived: Evil company corrupts good habits." (1 Corinthians 15:33)

So, in knowing that, try to surround yourself with company that welcomes correction and edification! And do not forget to also welcome correction yourself for by correction we improve.

REFLECTION

When you disagree with a friend, it's important to never lose sight of what is actually important. Sometimes when we are having an argument with a friend, we prioritise being right over our friendship. Remember to be wise in how you disagree yet understand that disagreements are a normal part of friendships. Ask yourself, how can I disagree with my friends in a more Godly manner?

Chapter Four

CHAPTER FOUR

Now we come to the last few verses of chapter 2. Paul elaborates even further on the theology behind his anti-Judaizer mentality. This level of detail is important for us to note because it tells us how important it is for the church to not be misguided by contradictory or false doctrine and the efforts that the church and we as its congregants should put into countering such teaching teachings. Paul writes the following verse:

"For if I build again those things which I destroyed, I make myself a transgressor. For I through the law died to the law that I might live to God.

Now you might read this and think to yourself, what's going on here, what is Paul saying? What Paul is saying is theology that has been the foundation of our faith for a thousand of years now. Paul is explaining to the Galatians that It would be contradictory for him to build again what he has destroyed, this is him referring to the law, stating that he has destroyed the teaching that the Jewish law is still relevant and necessary for salvation today. He say's this as reference to the previous verses, once again emphasis that going back on teachings makes you a transgressor. But what does he mean when he says, "I through the law died to the law that I might live to God."? To understand this verse, we have to address the concept of the law itself. You might be thinking of the law as something negative or something that was detrimental to early Christianity since Paul is so strongly against it. However, this is certainly not the case, we must understand that through the law we were saved. A great

Chapter Four

way of looking at this is understanding that the law paved the way for Christ and his crucifixion, by the foundations of the law and the followers of the law (Jews) Christ was able to come into this world to fulfill the law through his crucifixion and grant us salvation. So what Paul is referring to in verse 19 is actually dying with Christ and being reborn again through baptism. When we are baptised, we die to the law that we might live to God, thus granting us salvation. Paul even says this when he continues:

> "I have been crucified with Christ; it is no longer I who live, but Christ lives in me; and the life which I now live in the flesh I live by faith in the Son of God, who loved me and gave himself for me."

This beautiful verse holds wisdom that we should all strive to live by. Our sins, our passions and all the things that take us away from Christ have been crucified and now Christ lives in us. It is important, at all times, to understand that Christ is within us and lives

What the Fathers Say

"Just as by melting two candles together you get one piece of wax, so, I think, one who receives the Flesh and Blood of Jesus is fused together with Him. And the soul finds that he is in Christ and Christ is in him."
– St. Cyril of Jerusalem

People, Places & Things

For the beautiful verse 20, the original Greek actually has a single word for the term, "I have been crucified with" the Greek word is συνεσταύρωμαι (synestauromai) the literal definition of this word means to literally crucify someone together with someone else. Now Paul is not simply saying that he is sharing in the suffering of Christ on the cross, but rather he is saying that he understands that he too has accountability on the cross of Christ. He is saying that his old self, represented by his sins were crucified on that cross with Christ. As Christ's place on that cross is a fate that was meant for us, but He took it for us. So now we are reborn and have the option of salvation and a life without sin!

> **What the Fathers Say**
>
> The Cross, is wood which lifts us up and makes us great ... The Cross uprooted us from the depths of evil and elevated us to the summit of virtue.
> - St. John Chrysostom

within us. This is important in helping us avoid sin and also establishing that connection with Christ. When you are struggling with sin do not forget that Christ is in you and lives through you. When you want to find Christ, do not forget that Christ is in you and lives through you. Paul reiterates this in his first epistle to the Corinthians:

"But he who is joined to the Lord is one spirit with Him... Or do you not know that your body is the temple of the Holy Spirit who is in you, whom you have from God, and you are not your own?" (I Corinthians 6:17&19)

Knowing this, we must strive to live as Christ lived and as Christ is with us always, holding ourselves accountable for all that we do! Also respecting our bodies and living a life that is pleasing to Christ for our body is His also. Finally, I want us to look at the last line of verse 20. Paul explains to us that he lives by faith in the Son of God, "who loved me and gave himself for me." Remember that Christ said, "Greater love has no one than this, than to lay down one's life for his friends" and so Christ did so willingly for us, that we may be saved. However, Paul's choice of language here is intelligent and much more personal. Paul does not say that Christ died for us or died for you all (the Galatians). He says "Christ who loved me and gave himself for me" Paul emphasises Christ's crucifixion as being only for himself. This is the mentality that we all must have, that Christ is MY God and died for ME. In doing so, we make Christ's sacrifice personal, as it was a personal and perfect act of love.

The first way we can look at this is through the sins we commit throughout our lives. Ask yourself, would you commit certain sins if a priest or a parent was always with you? The answer is most likely no, so if that is the case, why then do we commit sins when God is with us always and within us. In addition to this, God being within us means that the sins we commit against our body we commit against Christ's body also. Now I do not want you to reflect on these things so that you can feel guilty, but so that together we all understand the weight of our role as Christians. When we are baptised, we are reborn and our flesh becomes Christ's flesh also, when we partake of the Communion, we see this occur physically as Christ's physical Body and Blood enters us. Now when we think of that, we might stop and worry, and think of all the times we sinned with God being within us or hurt our bodies. However, there is good news! Christ being within us means that He is always also available to us all. How many times in your life do you feel that you want to feel God but don't know how? You might go to church and try find Him there, but still do not feel his presence. You might listen to sermons and read the Bible and still not feel His presence. When you feel this way, push forward! For Christ being within you means He is always with you. No matter where you are, or how far you are from the church or how long it has been since you had communion, God is always with you. Look inward and you will find Him! This can be done through persistent prayer; speaking to God and telling him plainly, that you know He is within you, however you cannot feel His presence at that moment. God always hears our prayers and does not neglect those who cry out to him!

> **What the Fathers Say**
>
> "One must force himself to prayer when he has not spiritual prayer; and this God, beholding him thus striving and compelling himself by force, in spite of an unwilling heart, gives him the true prayer of the Spirit."
>
> - St. Macarius the Great

Never forget in the moments of your life when you feel like all hope is lost, when you are struggling with your faith and are confused about your purpose, that the Truth and Key to all things is within you, knocking on the door of your heart, waiting for you to open.

"And lo, I am with you always, even to the end of the age." – Jesus Christ (Mathew 28:20)

Reflection

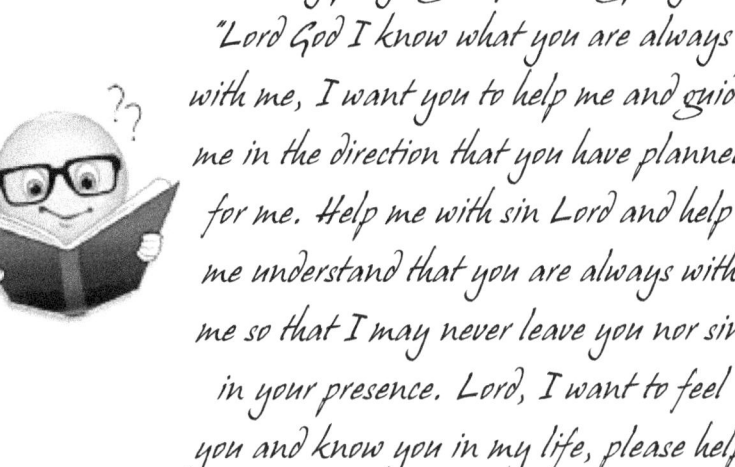

Let's try praying the following prayer: "Lord God I know what you are always with me, I want you to help me and guide me in the direction that you have planned for me. Help me with sin Lord and help me understand that you are always with me so that I may never leave you nor sin in your presence. Lord, I want to feel you and know you in my life, please help me to feel your prayers always. Amen."

Never forget in the moments of your life when you feel like all hope is lost, when you are struggling with your faith and are confused about your purpose, that the Truth and Key to all things is within you, knocking on the door of your heart, waiting for you to open.

"And lo, I am with you always, even to the end of the age."
- Jesus Christ (Mathew 28:20)

Chapter Five

Events

CHAPTER FIVE

Chapter 3 of the book of Galatians begins with Paul's signature passion against the Galatians for steering away from the faith. As is common throughout his epistle, Paul reveals his frustration to the Galatians over their actions. Paul's passion and fervour in his writing reveals to us his love for the church and the importance he places on not corrupting the gospel. Paul's reaction in itself tells us how important it is to remain steadfast in what we have been taught.

He begins by asking the Galatians, who has "bewitched" you? An expression revealing to us that Paul believes the Galatians must have been tricked through witchcraft in order to so easily be led astray. Obviously, Paul is exaggerating and simply using the word "bewitched" as a means of expressing his disappointment. But we have to understand the context in order to comprehend why he's using such strong language. Paul himself preached in Galatia, he spent time in Galatia and even previously explained how receptive they were to the Gospel. That's why he asks them, how can you "not obey the truth, before whose eyes Jesus Christ was clearly portrayed among you as crucified?" Paul is referring to the Gospel that the Galatians received willingly, his words are used as both praise and blame. He is telling them, that although Christ was not physically crucified in front them, their open receiving of the gospel made it as if he did. Just like us today, Christ's crucifixion is before eyes, we have seen Christ's crucifixion through our faith, we know that he died for us. Every time we stray from our faith and walk towards sin, we become just like the Galatians who strayed from the faith although Christ's crucifixion was before them.

Hence the praise refers to their willingness and openness to receive the gospel, however their blame is how easily they were deceived by the Judaizers, by reminding them of Christ's crucifixion he is reminding them that they are leaving the crucified Christ for the gospel that has been corrupted by the Judaizers. Paul continues:

> *"This only I want to learn from you: Did you receive the Spirit by the works of the law, or by the hearing of faith?"*

When Paul talks about receiving the Spirit, he is talking about the whole journey of Christianity (Receiving the gospel, being baptised, knowing salvation is attainable). He is asking the Galatians, through the works of the law, such as circumcision or keeping Jewish dietary laws, did you receive the Spirit or was it by faith? It was the hearing of faith that allowed them to

What the Fathers Say

"After gazing on the sun you seek a candle, after having strong meat, you run for milk!"

– St. John Chrysostom

Blind faith?

Should we do things without knowing why we do it? Is it not wrong to question? I thought we are all meant to have blind faith? Of course, blind faith in Christ is beautiful and recommended, however, regarding ritual and religious practice it is very important to know why you do the things you do in order to avoid being led astray. That was the issue with the Galatians, is that they did not seek to solidify their truth rather they accepted the methods of the Judaizers

> **What the Fathers Say**
>
> For no one turns away from God, except he who has first been deceived by some manner of good appearing in evil.
> – St. Gregory the Great

become Christians and attain salvation, so rightfully so, Paul is perplexed as to why they suddenly think that they have to take a step backward and focus on the works of the law. He tells them,

"Are you so foolish? Having begun in the spirit, are you now being made perfect by the flesh?"

What Paul means by this is that the Galatians began their journey of Christianity and faith through the spirit. In this context, spirit refers to their faith without needing to rely on works of the flesh. Paul then asked them, are the works of the law making you perfect now? The Galatians have already experienced the grace of the Holy Spirit, and it was done through their faith, why no would they go back to the works of law which cannot offer what the Spirit offers.

What St. Paul and St. John Chrysostom are saying actually relate to us more than you might think. I want you know to think about your moments as a Christian, your deep moments in prayer and the instances in your life that God might have spoken to you, and you felt His presence deeply. Did you remain in God's presence after that? Or did you turn your face from him and 'seek a candle' after already gazing upon the sun. What I mean to say is that so many moments in our lives, we might experience God, experience His presence, mercy and grace. But, unfortunately, after knowing the true happiness that we can only receive from our relationship with God, we still run back to the earthly things that give us temporary happiness. We forget what true freedom is with God and we run back to the slavery of the world. A way I can relate to our time today is our love for social media and the internet, unfortunately, although social media can have a lot of positives, it has been the cause of a mental health decline within our generation. Social media gives us this temporary happiness, this sense of excitement as we receive likes and endlessly scroll through videos. After indulging in so much social media throughout the day we might find ourselves lonely and unhappy. This is because we chose temporal things to decide our happiness, true happiness and peace can only come from God! And we having felt God and his presence and the joy that comes with a relationship with him, why do we run to these material and vain things. When you ever find yourselves in such a situation, remember the words of St. Paul, if you begin in the spirit, don't resort to the things of the flesh to make you perfect!

Continuing on to verse 4 and 5, Paul elaborates even further. He asks the Galatians if their suffering has been in vain since they

---

Religion in Galatia

Before St. Paul arrived to Galatia, the Galatians believed in the pagan "sky god" named Sabazios. When Paul arrived to Galatia, they were quick to reject their pagan gods and accept Christ as their saviour. Knowing this, you can see how upset Paul is at how quickly they also began to accept the teaching of the Judaizers when he praised them for being so receptive to the Gospel initially. But Paul understands that it is their lack of understanding and so he takes time to explain things to them.

know what to resort back to fleshly works of the law. What he means is that since you all suffered so much to be a Christian, is your suffering now useless since you now think that you should have been doing acts of the law this whole time? Paul is trying to put things in perspective for them, he is not telling them what to do and saying they must follow whatever he says. Paul is very passionate about teaching and educating what is right, not just simply saying "you must do this" without explanation. This is precisely why Paul has spent so much time on the topic. As well, we could learn from Paul's writing in our own life, it is very important that we know why we do the things we do in Christianity. Throughout your lives you will definitely meet people who asks why you do certain things in Christianity; you must be prepared to answer them. Hence, as a Christian you have a responsibility to know your own faith. Even someone in the church might come to and say, "I'm not doing this because I don't know why we do it!" you can't simply reply and say "You have to do it!" he definitely will not do it then. But if you understand why we do things within our church and why we have certain ritual and beliefs, then you can be like Paul and explain through education, that way people will definitely listen. Remember that our Orthodox faith is not focused on doing without understanding, although it might seem that way at times, the knowledge is there for us, we just have to take that step to understand why.

Chapter Five

Reflection

Orthodox Christianity is an ancient expression of faith with a plethora of rites, traditions and canons. It's such a shame that so many of us go on with our lives without truly understanding the wealth of knowledge and spiritual contemplations hidden in the traditions of the church. We are very lucky, however, to have priests and servants who are always willing to share their knowledge. It's important that we take time to ask questions and make it our goal to understand more about the faith.

Chapter Six

Abraham and the Judaizers

Earlier, I spoke about the intelligence of Paul's arguments and his ability to structure his points in a way that are proven to be effective. A prime example of this is within verse 6. Paul knows that to the Judaizers, the words of the scriptures and the law is extremely valuable to them. He knows that Abraham, the father of Jews, is held in high regard by the Judaizers. Hence, he uses the story of Abraham to explain his argument and to hold the Judaizers accountable. What he says is that Abraham, through his faith in God was righteous. It was not Abraham's deeds but his undeterred faith. Now why this is such a strong argument is because of the fact that Abraham was made righteous by God before the introduction of Jewish law. Paul is turning the Judaizers arguments against them, asking them: "If you need the works of the law to make you righteous and justified, why then was Abraham justified before the introduction of the law?"

In addition to this, Paul says that the scripture prophesied the idea that the faith would be for all people, not just the Jews. He backs up this argument by referencing God's message to Abraham:

> " *And the scripture, foreseeing that God would justify the Gentiles by faith, preached the gospel to Abraham beforehand, saying 'In you all nations shall blessed.' So then those who are of faith are blessed with believing Abraham.*"

Chapter Six

Paul uses the scripture that the Judaizers place so much emphasis on to show them their wrongdoing. This is a beautiful aspect of the way Paul brings forth his arguments, constantly backing himself up with the words of the scriptures. He has effectively put the Judaizers in a corner by using scripture against them, for if they disagree with him now after hearing these words, than they're disagreeing with the Bible. Hence, they're forced to agree. In this instance, Paul heavily mirrors Christ's discussion between the Pharisees, in which he would often use the Bible and their own beliefs to show them the correct way. Unfortunately, the Pharisees did not listen.

Faith over works? Saved by faith?

Now, as we go along, you might start to think that since Paul is placing so much emphasis on faith and only faith, are we thus saved only by our faith? Is that not what Paul is implying. He even says,

> **What the Fathers Say**
>
> Abraham is the father of all believers, not merely of those who are descendants of the flesh but of those who have the same faith.
> – St. Augustine

The Judaizers were quite crafty in their methods of deceiving the Galatians. Because the Galatians were made up of Gentiles, the Judaizers would explain to them that the law came before Christ and that's why it is so important. When the Galatians had confusions about why they required these old archaic laws, the Judaizers probably emphasised that since these laws are older than Christ and Christianity, they must be followed. The Judaizers used the Galatian's lack of scriptural knowledge to deceive them.

> *"Therefore, know that only those who are of faith are sons of Abraham"* (3:7)

What does it mean to be of faith? Is that all we need? To put it simply. No.

You might hear this term often from more Protestant traditions: this idea that we only need faith to be saved and "works" such as the sacraments are not necessary and are simply church tradition that does not save. You might even hear Pauls words throughout Galatians being used as evidence of this belief. However, it is important to know that this is definitely not the case and is not what Paul is saying. To understand what Paul is trying to say, we have to look once again at Jewish beliefs. A Jew is a Jew not because he believes in the religion of Abraham, but because he upholds the law. What this means is that to be a Jew, you must be circumcised (if you're a man), you must observe the sabbath and the feasts, and of course the commandments of all the Jewish law. To the Jews and especially the Judaizers, you were not a Jew unless you did all these things, you're faith was nothing without these things.

This of course, is different to Christianity. Our faith in Christ as our saviour and His resurrection is what makes us Christian. However, it does not end there. We know that simply believing in Christ does not guarantee us salvation. We know this because in his epistle, James dedicates a whole section to discuss faith without works. James states:

> *"What does it profit, my brethren, if someone says he has faith but does not have works?*

What the Fathers Say

The law leads to knowledge of sin and at length to the transgression of the law itself. It is thus with the knowledge and increase of sin that grace may be sought through faith.

– St. Augustine

Chapter Six

Can faith save him?" (James 2:14-15)

We need to always make sure that we never follow the extreme of either side. We must ensure that we don't follow the way of the Judaizers, by believing that our salvation is determined by our acts and rituals. Likewise, we also cannot believe that we can just by faith we will be saved. However, lets elaborate. You might ask, can't we just be nice to people and give to the poor and live a good Christian life without going to church and partaking in the sacraments? Well, the first issue with this way of thinking is the fact that we as Christians need a church and a community. Churches throughout the New Testament are Christian communities that were highly influential to the development of Christianity today. Galatia was a church! The concept of a church and a Christian community is all throughout the New Testament so we know that it is extremely important for us to be involved with a church community. In addition to that, the sacraments that we as Orthodox Christians are what have been prescribed to us by Christ. It was Christ who taught us to baptise; Christ who taught us to confess our sins to one another; Christ who taught us to marry and Christ who taught us communion. If by definition the word "Christian" means to be like Christ, then we must follow in Christ's ways and his teachings, because our great goal is to be one with Christ in all aspects. Therefore, as you read Galatians understand that Paul is specifically speaking about the Jewish works of the law that have been fulfilled by Christ.

> **What the Fathers Say**
>
> "He that believes in the Son has everlasting life." Is it enough, then, to believe in the Son,' someone will say, 'in order to have everlasting life?' By no means! Listen to Christ declare this himself when he says, 'Not everyone who says to me, "Lord! Lord!" shall enter into the kingdom of heaven'
> – St. John Chrysostom

REFLECTION

Be careful of those that you might meet in your life that might use the Bible to either justify sins or encourage you to do the wrong things. Remember that even Satan tried to tempt Jesus using the words of the Bible. So just because someone is using the Bible, that does not mean what they are saying is right. Just like the Galatians had St. Paul to correct them and direct them accordingly, we too have the Church and our priests to correct us and guide us just in case someone tries to lead us astray. Always fact-check what you hear with your priest or church leader!

Chapter Seven

CHAPTER SEVEN

Church Theology

Now in the verse 10-13 of Chapter 3, Paul delves deeply into some Christian theology. Together we will break down what Paul is saying and simplify the complex theology that he is presenting us. But before we do that, I'd like to speak about church theology and its role amongst the congregation. As you know, Paul addressed this letter to the entire church congregation of Galatia. The letter was not only read by the elders of the church, or behind closed doors in a board meeting. The letter would actually be read during, what we now call, the Liturgy of the Word. So, the entire church community would be seated and a deacon or priest would read Paul's letter to the whole congregation. Now this is important to keep in mind because what this tells us is that Paul did not direct any of the theology of his letters to only priests and deacons and/or learned members of the congregation. Paul was writing these letters, intending for everyone in the congregation to hear them. Today, some of us are under the belief that church theology is only for the "smart" people in the congregation, or the people in the congregation who are really spiritual. We might even think, only priests and some deacons should delve into theology while the rest of us should stay away because we might not understand it. This idea is definitely not true, church theology is for everyone! This is proven by Paul throughout his letters. Paul does not write his letters and shy away from deep theology or complex ideas because he worries that members of the congregation might not understand. Paul believed that everyone should know theology. Hence, we as well should not shy away from understanding the theology within our faith and beliefs.

Of course, not all of us can dedicate our time to studying at a theological college and reading as many spiritual books as we can. But my point is that we should not allow ourselves to be discouraged from theology or even think that theology is not for me just because I might think that it's too complicated for me. Remember that "God is not the God of confusion." With prayer God can help us understand.

The Curse of the Law

Now let's dive into the theology of what Paul is trying to say in verse 10. Paul says that:

"For as many as are of the works of the law are under the curse; for it is written, 'Cursed is everyone who does not continue in all things which are written in the book of the law, to do them.'"

When you first read this, you might think to yourself, "What? Why is Paul calling the law a curse? Was the law not the Old Testament rules that God gave the Jews?" You're right in thinking that. However, Paul isn't simply calling the law a curse. Paul is actually explaining to the Galatians how the law is a double-edged sword, so to speak. As you know, because of our fallen nature after humanity's conundrum in the garden, we were in a "fallen", OR you could say, cursed state. Because of this cursed state, the law was given to the Jews

> **What the Fathers Say**
>
> "He was made sin and a curse not on His own account but on ours... Cursed He was, for He bore our curses"
>
> - St. Athanasius of Alexandria

> **What the Fathers Say**
>
> The Law was a shadow of the good things to come, but now that Christ has come, we are no longer under the shadow, but in the full light of grace.
> – St. Irenaeus of Lyons

to keep them in line and prepare them for the coming of the Messiah, as I explained earlier. But Paul quotes Deuteronomy 27:26 which explain to the Jews that whoever does not continue in the ways of the law and all those commandments, they are cursed. But who can live their whole lives without breaking any commandments of the law? We were cursed and so we had to follow the law and yet the breaking of the law made us cursed also. Do you see what Paul is saying now? It's really a no-win situation. Now Paul continues and elaborates. He says, once again, that no one is justified by the law! And of course, this is true, the abidance of the law didn't grant us salvation. Paul quotes the old testament scriptures (Habakkuk 2:4), reiterating that the "just shall live by faith." And that it is the faith in Jesus Christ, who will come to save and justify us all!

That is the good news! While the curse of the law and the situation behind it might sound very doom and gloom, the good news is that Christ came for us, and so we can now attain salvation. Paul says in verse 13, that now "Christ has redeemed us from the curse of the law." Through Christ's death, we are no longer cursed. Of course, this is almost the entirety of Paul's argument throughout this Epistle. His point being that there is now good news, and we no longer must subject ourselves to the harshness of the Law. Christ subjected himself to the law and died for us so that we could be free! Paul even says this:

"Christ became a curse for us (for it is written, 'Cursed is everyone who hangs on a tree')"

Is Paul calling Christ cursed? Of course not, he is saying that he took the curse of sin; the curse of the law and died on a tree with that burden so that we may be saved. This line is very reminiscent to the entire Fraction to the Son from our liturgy, for example:

> *"We are the ones who sinned, and He was the one who suffered. We are the ones who were indebted to divine justice as a result of our and He was the one who paid off our debts for us... He went up on the cross naked to clothe us with the cloak of His righteousness"* – The Fraction to the Son, said at any time

Once again, just like Christ took what was bad about Paul and turned it into goodness; He also took our sins, our death sentence, and our curse of the law and turned it into salvation.

The Liturgy

The liturgies of the Coptic church and all apostolic churches serve as not only as a practise of partaking in the divine Eucharist, but also a reminder of our church theology. For example, in the Coptic Rite, the Liturgy of the Faithful begins with a catechesis. A catechesis is religious instruction for the purpose of explaining the faith. This catechesis is referred to as the Prayer of Reconciliation. Throughout this section of the liturgy, we are reminded of the entire process of salvation. Hence, the liturgy teaches us our theology every Sunday!

People, Places &Things

Chapter Eight

CHAPTER EIGHT

Events

Scripture as a foundation

Throughout the continuing verses within Chapter 3 of Galatians, Paul continues his theological commentaries. However, before we continue reading, I'd like to discuss Paul's method of explanation and discussion with the church of Galatia. I've spoken earlier about how Paul uses scripture in order to ground his arguments to the Judaizers with what they hold dear and abide by. Paul, throughout all his epistles, always grounds his words in the writings of scripture, anyway. However, within Chapter 3, which is not necessarily a big chapter, Paul refers back to the Old Testament six times. Not only does this emphasise Paul's knowledge of the scriptures but the fact that he is not allowing himself to speak without grounding any of his arguments with the scriptures. This is relevant to us today, many of us have encountered or will encounter situation where we have had to explain our faith, defend our faith and most importantly represent our faith. We can never accurately represent our faith if we are not well-versed in the Bible. Just like you would never go to a doctor who is not well-versed in anatomy, you also cannot expect to go through your life representing or defending Christianity without having read the Bible.

However, some say that they can't read the Bible because it's too difficult, or that they can't connect with the Bible because it can be boring at times. These are reasonable points but do not give you an exemption from reading the Bible. The Bible is not like any other book, we have to look at the Bible as a dynamic window into the world of God that is always changing depending on how we grow. You might not understand the Bible today, and so you spend years reading other books and improving your comprehension so that every year that goes past you understand more and more of the Bible. We also should always read the Bible with prayer, asking God to help us understand and to speak to us through the Bible. A good friend once told me that his dad had taught him a very beautiful habit to do whenever he opened the Bible to start reading. His Dad told him, just like Samuel, when he heard the voice of God called to him, responded with the words, "Speak Lord for your servant is listening." We too, should also get in the habit of saying that every time we open up our Bibles to read, that way we ground our reading session as a conversation between God and ourself. And remember that reading our Bible is a process, if you don't understand something or are discouraged by complicated writing, research, ask a priest or a friend and keep going. We have a whole lifetime to understand the words of the Bible.

What the Fathers Say

"As in paradise, God walks in the Holy Scriptures, seeking man."
– St. Ambrose of Milan

People, Places &Things

Abraham, Isaac and Jacob are often heard in our liturgical services through the following phrase: "In the bosom of our fathers Abraham, Isaac and Jacob."
The mention of these three prophets is often associated with salvation and heaven. Christ also refers to them in Matthew 8:11 "And I say to you that many will come from east and west, and sit down with Abraham, Isaac, and Jacob in the kingdom of heaven." The beauty of phrases such as this reveals to us the continuation of an ancient faith that has lasted for thousands of years. When we view ourselves in heaven it is not only humbling but encouraging to think that we will be up there with the forefathers of our faith. It is also beautiful to note that the actions of these great prophets have played a part in our salvation today!

Paul explains God's covenant with Abraham

Now in the following verses (15-18) Paul gives us an explanation on the covenant given to Abraham by God. But before we go into Paul's explanation, let's look at how Paul refers to the Galatians before he begins. Paul called the Galatians Brethren, and you might be asking yourself, "why does this matter? This is typical Biblical jargon…" and that is true, however, in the beginning of this chapter Paul referred to the Galatians as foolish. Verse one chapter three, the Galatians are foolish; verse 15 the Galatians are brethren. What this shows us, is Paul's love for his fellow believers in Christ, although he might have been angry or frustrated with the Galatians when beginning this chapter after he explained his point he reverts back to brethren. He did not let any disagreements with him and the Galatians break their bond and he is not prone to lingering anger. Sound familiar?

"For His anger is but for a moment, His favour is for life" Psalms (30:5)

Just like Paul and God in this Psalm, if we ever get angry or frustrated at our friends, let our anger be just for a moment and quickly come back to reconcile with your friend just like Paul did with the Galatians, calling them brethren.

Now back to Paul's explanation of Abrahams covenant, I find these verses very interesting because they feel as if Paul is giving us a sermon and breaking down the meaning of the Old Testament for us. Beginning with verse 15, Paul says:

Chapter Eight

"Brethren, I speak in the manner of men: Though it is only a man's covenant, yet if it is confirmed, no one annuls or adds to it."

You'll notice that Paul makes it clearly that he is speaking in the manner of men, what this means to us as modern-day readers is that Paul is saying, "let me put it simply for you" or "let me frame this in a way that everyday people will understand." He then goes on to do exactly that, explaining that any covenant, any agreement, once it has been confirmed, no one can add to it or remove it, simple as that. Of course, what he is speaking about is the covenant made with Abraham, Paul is implying that those in Galatia are attempting to change the original covenant that God made with Abraham. He elaborates on this by stating:

"Now to Abraham and his SEED were the promises made. He does not say, 'And to seeds,' as of many, but as of one, 'and to your seed,' who is Christ."

Verses such as these reveals to us more of Paul's clerical nature, serving the congregation by also providing them with commentary of the scripture. Now, in order to understand what Paul is trying to explain to us through this verse, we have to look back at the promises God made to Abraham. Throughout Genesis (Chapter 12, 13 & 24), God gives all these promises to Abraham and his "seed." Now, the Judaizers in Galatia have placed themselves as this aforementioned "seed" and have used the promises that God made to Abraham to puff themselves up over the Gentiles. In their eyes, they saw themselves as the seed of Abraham and that they were the true inheritors of God's promises. Paul is now refuting their claims and explaining to them that the word "seed" in the bible referred not to all the descendants of Abraham, but the One descendant of Abraham who is Christ. Paul proves this by saying that the verses in Genesis never used "seeds" as plural. In addition to this point, Paul is inferring that since God's promises to Abraham came before the Law, these promises thus overshadow the law, through Christ the promises of God have been fulfilled and the Law cannot overturn God's promises.

People, Places & Things

The Covenants of God

The definition of the word covenant means to enter into a formal agreement or contract. God has three main covenants in the Old Testament.

1. *The Covenant of Noah through the rainbow – A promise to never destroy mankind again*
2. *The Covenant of Abraham through circumcision – A promise to multiply the descendant of Abraham and bring forth salvation through his seed*
3. *The Covenant of Moses through the law – A promise to lead Israel and guide them to the promised land and through them, usher forth salvation*

The final covenant of God comes in the form of Jesus Christ, instituted for us through the last supper and his death. A covenant of salvation and eternal life.

CHAPTER EIGHT

REFLECTION

I was once having a conversation with someone about the reading of the Old Testament. He told me that he found the Old Testament boring and convoluted, he also stated "what's the point of reading he Old Testament, if the New Testament is the important part and concerns salvation." At the time I didn't have much of a response because I thought his points were valid. However, I now understand how important and vital the Old Testament is to our understanding of Christ and salvation. Never forget that the story of salvation begins with Genesis. God's plan for our salvation began from the moment Adam ate of the fruit, so it is important that we read the Old Testament to understand our own story of salvation and to understand the prophecies of Christ before His incarnation. Look at the wisdom of Paul, because of his understanding of scripture as a whole he is able to refute the Judaizers, so we too must also have an understanding of the Bible as a whole. Let's remind ourselves to spend time reading all books of the Bible so that we can be blessed with understanding!

Chapter Nine

CHAPTER NINE

The purpose of the Law

As we reach the end of Chapter 3, it seems that Paul finally addresses the question that would have likely been bugging the Galatians throughout his entire letter. So much has been said about the Law, so what is the purpose of the law then? Is it useless? Paul knew that this question would be asked and just like we discussed earlier, there is of course an answer. The Law is definitely not useless, and now Paul explains that to us clearly. He states to us that the reason the Law was given to Moses and the Jews is as a direct result of transgression. The Law served a temporary purpose until the Seed (Christ) comes and fulfills the promises of God. Through the coming of God salvation is granted the purpose of the Law has been fulfilled. He states that the Law was our "Tutor to bring us to Christ that we might be justified by faith. But after faith has come, we are no longer under a tutor."

The beautiful oneness of Christ's family

Finally, Paul holistically completes his third chapter to his Epistle to the Galatians in beautiful fashion. Verses 26-29 express a few of the most important lines said in the Bible and in history overall. To truly understand the impact of what Paul is about to say, however, we must look at the context of his time. St. Paul lived in an era of History in which all of humanity was placed under labels. What nationally you were and what gender you were determined your life before you could even live it. Life for a non-Roman citizen within the Roman Empire was extremely different to a Roman citizen. It is because of Paul's Roman citizenship that he was able to travel freely and escape a lot of tricky situations. Now imagine if you were a woman in that era. Once again life would be very different. Religion, gender, race, nationality and education all were factors determining someone's worth in St. Paul's world, and to an extent they still are in our world. Which is why the words of Paul changed everything, there are no other mass-produced texts from that era that state anything close to what Paul is about to say.

"For you are all sons of God through faith in Christ Jesus. For as many of you as were baptised into Christ have put on Christ. There is neither Jew nor Greek, there is neither slave nor free, there is neither male nor female; for you are all one in Christ Jesus"

In a world that is defined by labels, Paul breaks precedent and explains how Christ is the great equaliser. In Christ we are one. In Christ we are no longer segregated by our differences and instead we are united in our salvation. How beautiful is it that in a world where all things were decided by ones descriptors or labels, Christ's love filled Paul to understand that we are all one and the same, children of God destined, through salvation, to be with Him for an eternity. It is important that we remember these words when we go about our lives and fall into the trap of determining someone's value by labels. Always remember that we are one body in Christ, and knowing this is the first step to loving everyone around you.

Breaking Labels

In our day and age, people love to label everything including other people. Labelling

> **What the Fathers Say**
>
> *Difference of race or condition or sex is indeed taken away by the unity of faith, but it remains embedded in our mortal interactions, and in the journey of this life the apostles themselves teach that it is to be respected.... For we observe in the unity of faith that there are no such distinctions. Yet within the orders of this life they persist. So we walk this path in a way that the name and doctrine of God will not be blasphemed. It is not out of fear or anger that*

> we wish to avoid offense to others but also on account of conscience, so that we may do these things not in mere profession, as if for the eyes of men, but with a pure love toward God.
> – St Augustine

people seems to make us comfortable and gives us an idea of what other people are like. As you go about life, you will notice that the people you meet will ask you questions such as, "What are your political stances? What religion do you believe in? What background are you from? Do you believe in this idea? What is your sexuality?" All these questions stem from this desire to label people into categories. When we label people into categories, we can more easily judge them. We then have free reign to assume things about these people and say "oh well they did that because they are (insert label). Labels can be extremely dangerous as they push us to fall into the sin of judgement and this idea of segregation. However, it is extremely

Everybody's equal?

During the time of the early church, one of the most transformative and almost absurd aspects of Christianity was this idea of equality. The world at that time never truly comprehended a concept of equality and because of the church's emphasis on it, Christianity became revolutionary and transformative very quickly. The core tenants of modern civilisation are a direct result of the foundation of equality given to us by Christ and the church in the first century. Christianity changed the whole world and gave us the world as we know it today.

People, Places &Things

important to live life, not trying to separate ourselves and create barriers between us and others, but to break barriers and understand that our God, the God of Christians is the God of everyone. We should always remember the words of St. Paul as he tells us that in Christ there are no labels, we are all one. These words are beautiful as they bring us closer together in a world that is constantly putting barriers between people.

What the Fathers Say

We are all members of one body, and each member is essential for the whole. In Christ, we find our true unity, for He binds us together as one family.

– St. Gregory of Nyssa

REFLECTION

Let's make it our goal to stop viewing people using worldly labels. Let's try our best to see everyone as God's children and nothing else. Understand that when we judge others, we are judging God's children, and so we tell God, "I will take your place as judge!" Let's focus on ourselves and just see the good in others!

Chapter Ten

CHAPTER TEN

Events

Searching for slavery when we are free

Now as we enter Chapter 4 of the book of Galatians, Paul begins with a great analogy. Paul explains to us that a young man, who might be heir to a throne, before he comes of age is just like a slave. He is like a slave because he is still young and requires the wisdom of other to guide him and tell him what to do. He likens this scenario to humans who were under the bondage of the Law awaiting Christ. Paul says that we have always been heir's to the heavenly kingdom that God has prepared for us, but before Christ came we were like young children enslaved by sin and bound by the Law and now Christ has come and we can take up our rightful place in the kingdom.

"And because you are sons, God has sent forth the Spirit of His Son into your hearts, crying out, "Abba, Father!" 7 Therefore you are no longer a slave but a son, and if a son, then an heir of God through Christ."

Paul further elaborates, explaining that because we are sons of God, he has given to us the Holy Spirit and we can now cry out to him saying Abba, Father! We are no free, we are no longer slaves, we are heirs and we all have a place in God's kingdom. This is a beautiful follow up from the end of Chapter 3, as Paul previously mentioned under God there is no labels, so we are ALL heirs. Every single person in the world, no matter what gender, no matter what race, no matter where they are, they are an heir to God and they have a place prepared for them in the Heavenly Kingdom. How beautiful is it to know that God considers his heirs. How beautiful is it to know that there has been a place for us in Heaven since the foundations of the Earth were set. How beautiful is it know that God loves us and came down as a lowly Man to make sure that we are able to access the place and the kingdom that he set forth for us.

Another beautiful aspect of this verse is the word "abba". The word abba is a Hebrew term of endearment for father, and its presence in this verse reminds us that although Christ is King and creator of all, he does not want our formalities in calling him Father, rather he wants us to call him Abba. To put it in perspective, the word Abba is like a young child calling their father "daddy" today, it is a much more intimate and personal way of saying father, while also implying a physical and mental closeness. Similarly, our father, when said in the original Aramaic, used the word abba. This is a reminder to all of us that

What the Fathers Say

In calling God 'Father,' we acknowledge the intimate relationship He has with His children. This relationship is established through the Son, who reveals the Father to us.

– St. Irenaeus of Lyons

Our Father Who Art in Heaven

The Lord's prayer is a beautiful prayer given to us by Christ himself. The church regularly prays the Lord's prayer in every single service and prayer. The Lord's prayer is a reminder to us of our closeness to God, who is our Father even while He is presiding in Heaven. It is also a reminder to forgive; a reminder that our food comes from God and a reminder that we look forward for the coming of His kingdom. Next time you pray the Lord's prayer, think about the words!

> **What the Fathers Say**
>
> Do you see the compassion of the apostle? They were being corrupted. He trembles and fears. Therefore, he expresses this in a very solicitous manner, saying "I labored for you," as if to say, "Do not render such strenuous toils ineffectual for me." In saying "I fear" ... he has both stirred them up for a contest and directed them toward better hopes
> – St. John Chrysostom

God is not far from us, He is not a far of King in His heavenly Kingdom, but a loving Father who is near and dear to us, always around when we need him and never disappointing us. However, knowing this, we still might stray from God…

"But then, indeed, when you did not know God, you served those which by nature are not gods. 9 But now after you have known God, or rather are known by God, how is it that you turn again to the weak and beggarly elements, to which you desire again to be in bondage? 10 You observe days and months and seasons and years. 11 I am afraid for you, lest I have labored for you in vain."

Paul returns to reprimanding the Galatians about returning to the old ways of the Law through the misinformation that they have received. What Paul is asking, in context of the analogy, is why would you want to go back to bondage? You have been freed by Christ, you have known God why do you want to return and not know God? Of course he is talking about what the Judaizers have taught them, as through their teaching the Galatians thought they had to continue in all the practices of the Jews. Paul's perspective is that the Law was a bondage on account of our distance with God, now that we have God in our midst and Christ has died for us, why go back? Paul is agitated at their desire to return to the ways of the Law because he understands the freedom there is in Christ. The Galatians have even returned to observing days, and months and seasons, meaning that they have started to observe archaic Jewish feast days that no longer matter. For these feasts have been fulfilled by the new feasts, God gave

Chapter Ten

the Jews their feasts but they have now been succeeded by the feats of the church. For examples, Passover has now become Easter, while the original Jewish Pentecost, being the celebration of Moses receiving the Law, has now become the descent of the Holy Spirit. For this reason, Paul is agitated with the Galatians.

Now how does this relate to us in our modern world? Well how many times do we yank ourselves from Christ's grip in order to go out and seek the slavery of sin? We know that a life with Christ is true freedom and yet we turn our face from Him desiring that which does not satisfy. Paul is saying that if we did not know God, then to search for slavery and bondage is understandable, but having known God, how can we not hold ourselves to a higher standard?

Now is this to say that the Old Testament Law and the practices of the Jews in the Old

Agape

"Agape" is the Greek word for unconditional, selfless love, popularised by Christ and Christians. In the early Christian community, agape became a central concept in describing the love that believers were supposed to show towards one another, reflecting the love of God. This type of love was radically different from the more transactional or conditional forms of love common in the ancient world and led to significant admiration among non-Christians, contributing to the spread of Christianity.

Testament was incorrect or sinful? Of course not. As we spoke about earlier, the Law was given to the Jews to be observed during their time when salvation was not accessible to them. Salvation is now accessible so there are no longer in need of it. Paul ends with the line "I am afraid for you, lest I have laboured for you in vain." This line tells us a lot about St. Paul's character. He is filled with love for those he serves, and his harsh admonition of the Galatians does not stem from a desire to discipline, but from love. Paul loves the Galatians, and out of love he wants them to do the right thing. Paul loves Christ and out of his love for Christ he wants everyone to receive the message of the Gospel as it is! Not a corrupted message, nor an incorrect message, but the message of the Gospel.

Do you see the compassion of the apostle? They were being corrupted. He trembles and fears. Therefore, he expresses this in a very solicitous manner, saying "I labored for you," as if to say, "Do not render such strenuous toils ineffectual for me." In saying "I fear" … he has both stirred them up for a contest and directed them toward better hopes – St John Chrysostom

Reflection

But how do we achieve such love? Well, through spending time with Christ.

You might have noticed that if you spend a lot of time with someone, you begin to pick up a lot of their traits or habits. You might begin to speak the way they do or use certain words that they use. This is because we subconsciously pickup on the traits of the people we surround ourselves with. Now if I spend a lot of time with Christ and pray to Him, read His word and have moments of the day dedicated to Him, you will notice that you will also pick up on Christ's habits and love. In order to love like Christ, we must spend time with Him! So much so that His love overflows out of us and onto others.

Chapter Eleven

CHAPTER ELEVEN

Be like me and persevere

"Brethren, I urge you to become like me, for I became like you. You have not injured me at all. 13 You know that because of physical infirmity I preached the gospel to you at the first. 14 And my trial which was in my flesh you did not despise or reject, but you received me as an angel of God, even as Christ Jesus."

After St. Paul's pleading to the Galatians to return to the true words and the Gospel and reject outdated teachings, he encourages the Galatians to become like him. What does this mean?

Paul is not saying "become like me" out of a sense of pride or arrogance. He is not saying "I'm great, be like me." What he is saying is that he suffered with them and came down to their level to preach to them, now they should come up to his understanding of spirituality and understand him. Now also notice Paul's choice of words, as said earlier, after moments of reprimand, Paul also has moments of affection, using words such as brethren. Throughout this entire letter Paul is using his wisdom to make sure not to be too harsh but also not to be too easy on them so as to lose the true message of the Gospel.

Now Paul also mentions his physical infirmity. This physical infirmity is actually mentioned in other epistles, it seems that during Paul's mission he regularly suffered with illness. We know this because of the following verse:

Chapter Eleven

"And lest I should be exalted above measure by the abundance of the revelations, a thorn in the flesh was given to me, a messenger of Satan to buffet me, lest I be exalted above measure. 8 Concerning this thing I pleaded with the Lord three times that it might depart from me. 9 And He said to me, "My grace is sufficient for you, for My strength is made perfect in weakness." Therefore, most gladly I will rather boast in my infirmities"
(2 Corinthians 12:7-9)

Now Paul, being sick and suffering from an infirmity, did not allow it to hinder his service, but rather took it as a trial for humbling, as he says in the lines "lest I be exalted above measure." It seems this infirmity was flaring up during his preaching to the Galatians and he commends the Galatians for accepting him in his weakness neither despising him nor rejecting him. Paul is now calling to light the love that the Galatians showed them, once again reminding them of their good deeds so that they may be swayed to move away from incorrect teachings. In the following verses he actually questions the Galatians and asks them "where was this love and blessing that you showed me?"

"For I bear you witness that, if possible, you would have plucked out your own eyes and given them to me. 16 Have I therefore become your enemy because I tell you the truth?"

Paul even goes so far as to say that when he was with them, they were so obedient to his teachings that they would have plucked out their eyes if he had asked. Now, they view him as his enemy because he continues to tell them the truth. What we can surmise is that Galatians, after Paul left them and the

> **What the Fathers Say**
>
> See how again Paul addresses them by a name of honour, remembering to be gracious ... for just as continual flattery ruins people, so a continuously severe mode of speech hardens them. Therefore, it is good to maintain a balance everywhere.
> – St. John Chrysostom

What the Fathers Say

If the occasion demands it, a wise man will readily accept bodily infirmity and even offer his whole body up to death for the sake of Christ.
– St. Ambrose of Milan

Judaizers corrupted them, now see Paul as an enemy and speaker of false truth. How sad must it be for Paul, who worked so hard to send them the message of Love and the message of the Gospel only to be rejected once he leaves them and then be looked at as the enemy. Paul goes on to speak about the Judaizers and how they "zealously court" the Galatians, he explains that the Judaizers only want to woo them into this false sense of security and manipulate them into an exclusion. For we are now in communion with God, why should we want to exclude ourselves and be outside of his communion? Outside of his direct love? But Paul continues with his loving words, saying that he would like to be present with the Galatians once again and change his tone and sit with the Galatians in love bringing them back to Christ. Paul has no intention at all of giving up on the Galatians.

Holy Steps

Thanks to history, we have quite an accurate understanding of every location Paul visited and travelled to through his mission trips. The total distance St. Paul travelled comes down to 7325km! That's equivalent to 9 million steps! Now on top of all that on-foot travel, Paul was regularly writing letters and also building tents for income. Suffice to say, he sets the standard pretty high for Christian servants today!

People, Places &Things

Chapter Eleven

Perseverance is what we all as Christians will have to experience throughout the entirety of our lives for Christianity is a struggle, a beautiful struggle. Just as we struggle through the woes of life so must we struggle with the ups and downs of our spirituality. But of course, it is never about how many times we fall but about how many times we get up. This process of getting up is perseverance, and it is one of the greatest lessons we can learn from St. Paul. As you can see, Paul won't give up the Galatians easily and neither should we give up on our services, friends, family and own spiritual life. When you pick up a service to do for God, or a mission, it is important to not give up. When you pray and you fail to establish a routine, it's important to not give up. When you're friends and family are doing things that hurt you or themselves it's important that you don't give up telling them the truth and praying for them. Finally, always remember that in the truth of the Gospel, you too must also be true to yourself and others around you. Just like Paul is not attempting to "make okay" what the Galatians are doing neither should you "make okay" the wrong things that you do or see others do. Be true as the Gospel is true. Persevere and never give up, knowing the Christ is with us always and is always nearby to help, however, he can't help us if we give up!

> **What the Fathers Say**
>
> Pray as though everything depended on God. Work as though everything depended on you.
>
> – St. Augustine

REFLECTION

Let's take inspiration from St. Paul and be inspired to never allow ourselves to feel down and unmotivated on account of our sins. This week let's focus on consistency in our prayer, Bible reading and quiet time. If we fall, we will get back up again. Just as St. Paul persevered, let us also persevere!

Chapter Twelve

CHAPTER TWELVE

Christ as the fulfilment of the story of Abraham

Now, before we can continue, it is important to understand the Old Testament context that Paul is about to give to us. We will begin with a recap of Abraham's story.

Who is Abraham?

As you know, Abraham is the father of Judaism and Christianity, since, through Abraham, we received Judaism, the Law and now Christ. Within the Orthodox church services, we regularly reference Abraham, Isaac and Jacob as the forefathers of our faith. They are the prophets that struggled for God and through them Christ came and granted us salvation. But who is Abraham?

Abraham was a simple righteous man whom God chose to father the children of Israel. God promised Abraham that the nation of Israel will be born of him and that his descendants will be like the stars. God also promised him land for his descendants to live and thrive on. Now Abraham was perplexed and confused about God's promise as he and his wife were unable to have children, and they were both already well into their years. But God promised Abraham multiple times and assured him that he will have descendants and that he will be father to a great nation. His wife, Sarai, was not convinced, she approached Abraham and said to him, "Since you cannot bear any children with me, marry my maidservant and bring forth a child from her as I want you to have an heir." Sarai's maidservant was Hagar and Abraham did as

Chapter Twelve

Sarai said and he had a child with Hagar and they named him Ishmael.

Now the issue here is that God had already promised Abraham a child, Abraham and his wife were unable to wait and so they took things into their own hands and decided to work around God's promise. Eventually Sarai gave birth to a child and they named him Isaac, and through Isaac the nation of Israel arises leading all the way to Christ. Ishmael, however, left Abraham's kingdom and made his own nation. Isaac was the child of promise but not Ishmael.

Now this all might sound quite harsh for Ishmael, but God did look after Ishmael and gave him land and a great nation. But that nation was not Israel, nor did that nation bring forth a messiah, as Ishmael was born of the flesh and not of promise.

Which leads us into what Paul is now saying, using the story of Abraham and his two sons as an example. St. Paul begins by saying, those of you who desire to be bound under the Law, let's have a look at the Law and see what it really says.

"For it is written that Abraham had two sons: the one by a bondwoman, the other by a freewoman. 23 But he who was of the bondwoman was born according to the flesh, and he of the freewoman through promise, 24 which things are symbolic. For these are [g]the two covenants: the one from Mount Sinai which gives birth to bondage, which is Hagar— 25 for this Hagar is Mount Sinai in Arabia, and corresponds to Jerusalem which now is, and is in bondage with her children— 26 but the Jerusalem above is free, which is

> **What the Fathers Say**
>
> *Be patient and wait upon the Lord, for He will come and will not delay. Let your heart be strengthened, for the Lord is faithful and His promises are true.*
> – St. Ignatius of Antioch

What the Fathers Say

We look for the kingdom that is to come, according to the words of Jesus, who instructed us to wait with patience and readiness, knowing that the times and seasons are in the Father's hands.
– St. Justin Martyr

the mother of us all."

Now this might seem quite confusing, but let's break down what Paul is saying. He refers to the story of Sarai and Hagar as an allegory, not because it did not actually happen, but that the meaning of the story is also relevant to what is happening at the moment to the Galatians. Paul is likening the Galatians who wish to be under the confines of the law as akin to the nation of Ishmael. For the nation of Ishmael were not God's chosen people and not a nation of promise and therefore did not have rights to Jerusalem. Likewise, the Galatians are choosing the earthly archaic law rather than the new covenant of God, they are choosing to be sons of the Earth rather than sons of the New Jerusalem. God is no longer concerned with the earthly Jerusalem, rather he has formed for us the New Jerusalem which is heaven, a kingdom which has been prepared for us since the foundations of

Polygamy in the Old Testament

You might be thinking, why would God allow polygamy to occur in the Old Testament? Polygamy is not the desire of God and was not God's intended marriage. Unfortunately the Old Testament patriarchs being imperfect fell into the sinful state of polygamy. Having multiple wives, however, does not work out well as is the case for Abraham. Once Christ comes along he corrects the standards and explains very clearly that marriage must be between one man and one woman!

People, Places &Things

Chapter Twelve

the Earth. Why then would we choose the earthly Jerusalem? Why then would we choose the Earthly laws? Why choose the nation of Ishmael when we are the Children of Isaac? Paul also mentions Mount Sinai and compares Mount Sinai to Hagar. Mount Sinai is significant because it is where Moses received the 10 commandments. This event is a symbol of the Old Covenant, however, that does not mean that 10 commandments no longer apply, rather it means that we have received a new updated covenant, so why go back to the old one? This New Covenant is Christ who, of course, came down and granted us salvation.

Now, notice how Paul refers to the current Jerusalem as in bondage. This is because, as you know, the earthly Jerusalem has never been free from occupation, wars and violence since the time of Christ. Similarly, the children of the earthly Jerusalem, the modern Jews, are also still in bondage, for they are still waiting for the messiah without a nation, without a temple and without a high priest. This is fascinating because when St. Paul wrote this epistle, Jerusalem was still in bondage to the Romans and till this day it is still in bondage to political turmoil and violence. All this turmoil is because the Messiah has come, Christ has come! And, once again, the earthly Jerusalem no longer matters, instead we should be focused on Heaven and our place in the next world.

Paul finishes chapter 4 with the emphasis that once again we are now the children of promise. We are now worthy of the kingdom and salvation and it is in our grasp so long as we choose it. He refers back to scripture which states:

> "Cast out the bondwoman and her son: for the son of the bondwoman shall not be heir with the son of the free woman."

Just like Ishmael is not the heir, the Jewish law is not the way to salvation, rather Christ has become the way to salvation.

Now our thinking is sometimes like the pharisees. At times we are so focused on this world, this place, our job, our clothes, our studies, our money, our material possessions. Sometimes, we seek God exclusively for these worldly things. We pray to God in the hopes that he will give us a great earthly life. Of course, God cares about everything in our life, but He knows there is so much greater after our time on this earth is done. Do we know that? Or are we so focused on everything in this world that we forget about the next one? Now I am not only talking about people who

---

The Jewish Messiah

Certain Jews of Christ's time such as the Pharisees had a skewed expectation of who the messiah would be. They believed that a Jewish man, born of the line of David, would come and be anointed with the holy anointing oil and rule the Jewish people during the Messianic Age. Their expectations of this messiah was one of an Earthly liberator who would restore the power of Judaism and make them a great nation once more. Christ did not do this but rather He did something so much better; He liberated us from death and promised everyone the Eternal Kingdom.

focus on worldly pleasure, even those of us within the church can also be focused too much on the earthly side of everything. Some Christians are so religious that they forget to be spiritual. Let us never forget that we sojourners in this world waiting for the day that the Lord will take our hand and guide our souls to his beautiful and glorious Kingdom in which there will be no more suffering and no more pain.

In the times of the early church there was a common saying that I believe we should try to always remember today. Memento Mori which is Latin for "remember your death." At times when we get caught up in the craziness of this life, we forget to remember that one day were all going to die. We forget to remember that we have a place set out for us, that we must always have our mind on our death so when the day comes we are ready.

> *"Therefore keep watch, because you do not know on what day your Lord will come. 43 But understand this: If the owner of the house had known at what time of night the thief was coming, he would have kept watch and would not have let his house be broken into. 44 So you also must be ready, because the Son of Man will come at an hour when you do not expect him. (Matthew 24:42-44)*

REFLECTION

In the times of the early church there was a common saying that I believe we should try to always remember today. Memento Mori which is Latin for "remember your death." At times when we get caught up in the craziness of this life, we forget to remember that one day were all going to die. We forget to remember that we have a place set out for us, that we must always have our mind on our death so when the day comes, we are ready.

Therefore keep watch, because you do not know on what day your Lord will come." (Matthew 24:42-44)

Chapter Thirteen

CHAPTER THIRTEEN

Rejoice! For you are free

Now we begin looking at Chapter 5 of Paul's epistle to the Galatians. In this chapter, Paul reiterations the notion that we must rejoice in our freedom, rather than returning to the bondage that we were previously subjected to. You will notice as well as you read this chapter that the tone of Paul's writing is filled with such fervent passion and frustration. Now this frustration is not directed at the Galatians in anger, but it is because of his love for them. Paul, who truly understands the freedom of Christ is saddened by the desire of the Galatians to actively choose slavery over freedom. He begins this chapter by commanded them to "stand fast" in the liberty by which Christ has given them and not return back to bondage. Which is a reminder to all of us as we live our day to day lives, to understand the freedom that we have received through Christ and not to return back to our former ways. While we might not struggle with the desire to return back to the Law of Moses, we do struggle with the desire to return to the slavery of sin. When we read this chapter we must remind ourselves that sin is slavery and we have freedom now, we must never again desire less than that which is freedom through Jesus Christ.

Paul continues and says quote a confronting statement, which is precisely what the Galatians need to hear:

"Indeed I, Paul, say to you that if you become circumcised, Christ will profit you nothing. And I testify again to every man who becomes

Chapter Thirteen

circumcised that he is a debtor to keep the whole law."

Now this is quite a confronting statement, but what does Paul mean?

Going back to the Judaizers; the Judaizers focused mainly on maintaining the Jewish cultural practices of the Law so as to retain Jewish superiority within Christianity. Circumcision being a key aspect of the Law, they pushed the gentile Galatians to practice circumcision as well. Paul, thus, says well if you practice circumcision you are also indebted to practice all other aspects of the law. Now we know that law is filled with a lot of difficult practices (Observation of certain feasts, laws of dress and laws of marriage) things that cannot apply to the gentiles and have no longer a need to apply to the gentiles. Paul is therefore emphasising to them that there is not even a point of overblowing certain aspects of the law when you are not even able to fulfill all aspects of the law! Paul is pushing the gentiles to see their futility in their attempts to maintain the archaic Law of Moses which Christ has fulfilled.

We must emphasise once again, that the Law of Moses was established by God to bring forth the Messiah. Now that the Messiah has come, there is a new law, the Law of Christ. The previous law has served it's purpose and Christ has given us a new Law, to live with love according to His divine words.

Paul elaborates on this idea saying:

"You have become estranged from Christ, you who attempt to be justified by law; you have fallen from grace. For we through the Spirit eagerly wait for the hope

> **What the Fathers Say**
>
> With freedom did Christ set us free; stand fast therefore. Have you wrought your own deliverance, that you run back again to the dominion you were under before? It is Another who has redeemed you, it is Another who has paid the ransom for you.
> – St. John Chrysostom

> **What the Fathers Say**
>
> Observe in how many ways he leads them away from the error of Judaism; by showing, first, that it was the extreme of folly for those, who had become free instead of slaves, to desire to become slaves instead of free; secondly, that they would be convicted of neglect and ingratitude to their Benefactor, in despising Him who had delivered, and loving him who had enslaved them; thirdly, that it was

of righteousness by faith. For in Christ Jesus neither circumcision nor uncircumcision avails anything, but faith working through love."

Now to put this in context, we have to understand that the Galatians were led to believe that if they did everything correct according to the words of Jesus, they still would not be saved unless they were circumcised. This of course, is not what we as Christians believe and explains the frustration that Paul is experiencing. We are called as Christians to practice our faith "working through love." Paul further explains his frustration by commending the Galatians and saying, "You ran well, who is hindering you that you should not obey the truth?" Paul is emphasising that he knows that external influences (the Judaizers) are pushing the Galatians down the wrong path and it does not come from them originally as he knew they were doing the right thing. In the following verse, Paul exclaims that what they have been taught definitely does not come from God who calls them. He says this to affirm to them that what they are doing is not God's will, but rather the will of earthly people.

Paul then says, "A little leaven leavens the whole lump." Leaven refers to yeast. Paul's meaning here is pretty much, "One bad fruit spoils the bunch." This saying reveals his intention for taking such a hard stance against the Galatians as he knows that if this "leaven" is allowed to spread amongst the church it can grow and ruin the entire church. This thus justifies his anger in the following verses. Before he continues in his criticism of the Judaizers he encourages the Galatians, affirming that that he has confidence in them to remain on the right track and that God will Judge the Judaizers due to their actions of steering the Galatians from the true faith. Paul is practising what he was saying earlier, practising his faith "through love." We must understand that Christianity without love is void and Paul is showing this in his writing; while he is firmly against that which is wrong he firmly gives love through wisdom to the Galatians as he understands that true Christianity is centred and grounded in love. When Paul reminds them that the Christian faith is faith working through love, he is emphasising that as long as we are grounded in the love of Christ we will not stray to other teaching. What can we take from this? Well, we must always remind ourselves that Christ has made us free and we should rejoice in this freedom. However, we must also remember that if we stop loving others and stop practicing a faith that works through love, we will very easily fall back into slavery.

impossible. For Another having once for all redeemed all of us from it, the Law ceases to have any sway.
– St. John Chrysostom

Freedom of Expression

The Abrahamic religions except for Christianity are all tied with culture and cultural practice. You could even argue that all religions are tied with culture except Christianity. An example of this is the way Coptic Christians might worship God compared to Ethiopian Christians. Coptic Christians only use a cymbal and triangle in their liturgical practices, while Ethiopians use a drum and almost dance in their worship. Similarly, these methods are completely different to a Christian practising in Europe. It is exactly these differences that remind us that in Christianity is the truth, for Christianity is compatible with all.

People, Places &Things

REFLECTION

Ask yourself, am I truly practising my faith with love, or am I turning my faith into rules? Not to say that Christianity does not have rules, but that the obedience of those rules comes as a natural consequence of Christ-like love. Christianity is the freedom to now be what God originally intended for us through the Blood of Christ.

Chapter Fourteen

CHAPTER FOURTEEN

Love Fulfills the Law

All this talk of love finally leads us to the next point Saint Paul is trying to make, that love fulfills the Law! But before Paul makes the point of Love fulfilling the law he mentions this:

"And I, brethren, If I still preach circumcision, why do I still suffer persecution? Then the offense of the cross has ceased."

The context behind this statement is that some of the Judaizers actually went as far as to that Paul is the one who actually preaches circumcision but is hypocritical as he changes his mind. It seems they might have made this claim off of the fact that Paul circumcised Timothy in Acts 16. Take note of the specific language Paul uses, however, he explicitly states "If I still preach," he is emphasising here that he never preached that anyone should be circumcised and if that was in fact the case, why would he still be suffering persecution from the Judaizers? Paul circumcised Timothy because he knew that the circumcision of Timothy would lead to better results when preaching to the Jews. He did not preach that that circumcision was required, but rather he circumcised him for the sake of the service. We see Paul's sentiment behind this logic in 1 Corinthians 9:20-22:

" and to the Jews I became as a Jew, that I might win Jews; to those who are under the law, as under the law, that I might win those who are under the law; 21 to those who are without law, as without law (not being without law toward God, but under law toward Christ), that I might win those who

are without law; 22 to the weak I became as weak, that I might win the weak. I have become all things to all men, that I might by all means save some."

We understand, thus, that Paul "levelled" with the people he would preach to. This is something we do all the time. When we deal with young children we speak like children to them so that they might more easily listen to us. When we speak to a principal or police officer, we speak to them more formally so that we show professionalism and seriousness. However, Paul never preached the things that he did not believe were correct, which is what he is emphasising. It is important that when we seek to serve and persuade others, we come down to their level and are inclusive in our ways, without, of course committing deeds that are sins or that take us from God.

> **What the Fathers Say**
>
> *Paradise is the love of God, wherein is the enjoyment of all blessedness.*
> – St. Isaac the Syrian

The Kiss of Peace

Christianity is all about loving each other and avoiding harbouring any hatred or bitterness for each other. This is so important for Christians that even in the Liturgy, you are not permitted to have communion if you there is an unsolved dispute between you and another member of the church. You must first attempt to make amends before having communion (Matthew 5:24). This is also reflecting in the Kiss of Peace that all apostolic Christians partake of in the Liturgy to ensure that the congregation is at peace with one another.

What the Fathers Say

What need is there for the holy apostle to make use of the law, if the new covenant is foreign to the old legislation? He wants to show both covenants are from the one Lord. They are best perceived as sharing the same intent. The fulfillment of the law is through the love of one's neighbour, because love is that which effects the perfect good. He therefore says that love is the fulfilling of the law

– St. Epiphanius of Cyprus

The following verses, St. Paul now reminds the Galatians of the true purpose of the Gospel. The message of love, of course! He explains that now that Christ has given us liberty, we should not use that liberty to enjoy a life of worldly desires and satisfying the flesh. Rather, we ought to use this liberty to love and serve one another. Paul then makes the beautiful claim that:

> *"For all the law is fulfilled in one word, even in this: "You shall love your neighbour as yourself.""*

Such a beautiful statement, that truly underlines the crux of our lives as Christians! The whole purpose of the law was that we may now enjoy the newfound freedom Christ has given us and to love our neighbours. This reveals to us how from days of Moses, God's plan for humanity was to live together in love and be like Him! And when we do that, we are fulfilling the overall purpose of the law.

With that final understanding, Paul, at last, ends his explicit commentary on the Law of the Old Testament, choosing now to spend the rest of the epistle encouraging the Galatians by explaining to them how Christian ought to act.

So you see now that through Christ, God has taken all that was hard, difficult and rough in the law and has perfected it for us and given us Christ's law. Christ's law has given us freedom and rest.

"Take My yoke upon you and learn from Me, for I am gentle and lowly in heart, and you will find rest for your souls. For My yoke is easy and My burden is light." (Matthew 11:29)

Chapter Fourteen

The pain of circumcision has become the refreshment of baptism. The suffering of innocent animals has become the joy of us partaking of Communion. The exclusivity of a single day of rest has been perfected so that all days may become rest for us. How wonderful and merciful is our God! Truly Christ's yoke is easy and His burden is light! I want you now to think of all the good things and blessings God has given you in your life and take a moment to thank Him. Too often we ask God for so much, forgetting to thank Him for the abundance of things He Has already given us.

> **What the Fathers Say**
>
> Do not seek the perfection of the law in human virtues, for it is not found perfect in them. Its perfection is hidden in the Cross of Christ.
> - Hesychius the Priest

Reflection

I want you now to think of all the good things and blessings God has given you in your life and take a moment to thank Him. Too often we ask God for so much, forgetting to thank Him for the abundance of things He Has already given us.

Chapter Fifteen

CHAPTER FIFTEEN

Now that St. Paul has clearly refuted the arguments of Judaizers, he now dedicates the rest of this epistle to spiritual words that edify the Galatians. Once again, revealing the wisdom of Paul. As stated previously, he regularly switches between firm instruction and kind wisdom in his writing style. But the wisdom he is about to give is not just any wisdom, it is a wisdom that has resonated with all Christians throughout hundreds of years and continues to resonate today.

You have probably heard about the advice he is now about to share. He refers to it as the Fruit of the Spirit. Which is an explicit explanation on what types of behaviours or traits we should endeavour to constantly employ as Christians, as these behaviours are a "fruit" of the spirit. But what do we mean by fruit?

The fruit here represents an analogy, one that Christ regularly used in His own sermons. The analogy is that people are like trees, a good tree yields good fruit and a bad tree yield bad fruits. Hence, when Christ refers to false prophets he says, "You will know [a false prophet] by their fruits" (Matthew 7:16). Which means that a false prophet will not produce good outcomes, therefore, by the outcome of his work, you will know of his falsehood. Similarly, this can be applied to the opposite case, we know that a good worker is a good worker because he produces... you guessed it, good work! So, when Paul refers to the fruit of the spirit, he is referring to the fruits of a person who is being led by the spirit.

Chapter Fifteen

The Works of the Flesh

Before St. Paul explains what the Fruit of the Spirit are, he makes it very clear to us that we as human beings are in a constant battle between spirit and flesh, think of Matthew 26:41 "The spirit indeed is willing, but the flesh is weak."

We all understand that sometimes what we want to do, especially spiritually, is weighed down by the desires of our flesh. In this case, Christ was instructing the disciples to pray but they kept on succumbing to the flesh and falling into sleep.

However, Paul is not just talking about giving into the needs of the body, such as sleep, Paul is talking about our body's desire for sin. He makes it clear, that we must be walking with our spirit and not walking with our flesh. But what does this

> **What the Fathers Say**
>
> *Desire only God, and your heart will be satisfied.*
> – St. Augustine

Hamartia

You might know the word hamartia from studying Shakespearean or Greek tragedy in English class, but did you know that hamartia is the Greek word for sin in the New Testament. This is interesting as the literal definition of hamartia means: to miss the mark. Hence, to sin is to fall short of our true purpose!

Our "mark" being a pure and undefiled life with Christ. Remember hamartia whenever you think of your sins!

> **What the Fathers Say**
>
> Let us behold Him in spirit, and look with the eyes of the soul to His long-suffering will. Let us consider how gentle He is toward all his creation.
> – St. Clement of Rome

mean? Well in all aspects of life, we practice self-control, right? You would not be able to function if you decided to just give your body what it wants every day. For example, your body does not want to wake up at 6 am and go to work/school, however, you push through because you know that school/work is important. Similarly, your body might want to eat 12 donuts in one sitting, but you know that you can't do that as it's not healthy, and it'll probably hurt your stomach after. Think about what type of person you would be if you were to just live off of what your body desires on a day-to-day basis, you probably would not be a functioning member of society.

Similarly, we experience the same battle in our own spiritual lives. Spiritually we might not want to pray but we must push ourselves. We might not want to go to church but we must push ourselves! This is what St. Paul is talking about, that we are Christian you live a life based on what our spirit needs not based on our flesh. To make it clear to us, he goes through and lists all the sins that are works of the flesh and explains that the regular practice of such things will lead us away from inheriting the Kingdom of God.

> *"Now the works of the flesh are evident, which are: adultery, fornication, uncleanness, lewdness, idolatry, sorcery, hatred, contentions, jealousies, outbursts of wrath, selfish ambitions, dissensions, heresies, envy, murders, drunkenness, revelries, and the like; of which I tell you beforehand, just as I also told you in time*

past, that those who practice such things will not inherit the kingdom of God."

I would like to focus on Paul's concluding words here, "those who practice such things will not inherit the Kingdom of God." We can sometimes fall into the trap of focusing too much on the mercy of God and forgetting that sin drives us away from God and leads us into a state in which we cannot inherit the Kingdom. Remember the words of St. Paul in Philippians 2:12 "work out your own salvation with fear and trembling;" While God is of course abundant in mercy and grace, our salvation is something that requires us to work for it, with fear of sin and the isolation form God that it yields.

St. Paul is emphasising that the works of the flesh draw us from God. The world wants us to focus on the works of the flesh, they encourage all the works that Paul spoke against. The world tells us things such as, "Live your life! Have fun and enjoy! Do what your body desires!" Not understanding that those who live yielding to the desires of the flesh, not only end up being unhappy, but cannot inherit the things which are Godly!

St. Augustine was a great saint because he spent his youth away from God and he realised just how superficial and unsatisfying such a life his. Once he truly found God he dedicated his life to him! How much more is expected of us who have been blessed to know God and have the church from such a young age. As you go through your life, never forget that nothing can satiate you other than the life of God, for us being made in the image of God cannot be separate from God!

> **What the Fathers Say**
>
> Men are often called intelligent wrongly. Intelligent men are not those who are erudite in the sayings and books of the wise men of old, but those who have an intelligent soul and can discriminate between good and evil.
> – St. Anthony the Great

REFLECTION

Ask yourself: "How often am I partaking in the works of the flesh? How much of my life is being lived with the desire for comfort? Think about your day to day to living. Are you driven by what your body wants to do? Rather than what is good for your spiritual life. Something I like to do is always remind myself that I only have one life and one chance at salvation. Knowing this, we understand that every action we take right now impacts our after life! So why then do we spend so much time away from God? Why then do we spend so much time sinning and indulging in the pleasures of the body when we know that nothing will ever satiate our desires except God. As you go through your life, never forget that nothing can satiate you other than life with God, for us being made in the image of God cannot be separate from God!

Chapter Sixteen

The Fruit of the Spirit

Now we can finally talk about the famous Fruits of the Spirit. Remember that what St. Paul is explaining here is what the fruits of a person walking by the spirit are. So, we as Christians must hold the following verse close to our heart. If we are striving to walk by the spirit, then we know that our fruits must be the following:

" But the fruit of the Spirit is love, joy, peace, longsuffering, kindness, goodness, faithfulness, gentleness, self-control. Against such there is no law."

Love

Of course, Paul begins the first fruit of the Spirit as love! How can we do anything without love! Should we have any of the other fruits, they must be meaningless without love. For love is the foundation of who we are as Christians.

Joy

Paul states that we must have joy but also says that we must experience longsuffering. Can we be joyful yet also suffer? Of course! Remember that a life with Christ is pure joy, not because it is a life of comfort, but because in discomfort our faith and trust in Christ gives us peace, the true peace that gives us joy!

These things I have spoken to you, that My joy may remain in you, and that your joy may be full (John 15:11)

So, a person walking in the spirit is a person that is joyful because he knows Christ, loves him and trusts in him and that is the foundation of his joy.

Peace

A Christian should always be filled with peace! Walking in the spirit gives us a sense of peace because we know that everything is going to be okay. Because we know that Christ came and died for us and told us not to worry. To walk in the spirit means to not worry about quarrels, to not instigate drama or fights but to be a being of peace!

Longsuffering

Longsuffering is a difficult one that I think sometimes gets brushed over when we discuss the fruits of the Spirit. It is important to understand that you as Christians are not called to a life of comfort! But Christ told us

What the Fathers Say

What deserves to hold the first place among the fruits of the Spirit if not love? Without love other virtues are not reckoned to be virtues. From love is born all that is good.

– St. Jerome

Apples and Oranges

Fruits are mentioned all throughout the Bible. The story of man's fall and salvation even begins with a fruit. But why fruit? Well fruits give life! So long as the tree is a good tree, it will bear good fruit, and that fruit will give you sustenance and life. Because of this understanding of fruits, fruits are often used as a symbol of the naturally occurring deeds that come out of being Christ-like and loving. That is why Christ cursed the Fig tree as it was a healthy tree but produced no fruit! Likewise we must be weary of being in a position in which we can bear good fruit but we choose not to.

What the Fathers Say

But let us consider whether He has goodness in Himself, since He is the Source and Principle of goodness. For as the Father and the Son have, so too the Holy Spirit also has goodness. And the Apostle also taught this when he said: 'Now the fruit of the Spirit is peace, love, joy, patience, goodness.' For who doubts that He is good Whose fruit is goodness? For 'a good tree brings forth good fruit'
– St. Ambrose of Milan

that as Christians we will suffer. But the good news is that it's okay to suffer! Christ suffered! He knows our pain and he is with us every step of the way.

In the world you will have tribulation; but be of good cheer, I have overcome the world.
(John 16:33)

Kindness

Kindness is a reflection of love, true love cannot exist without kindness. Ask yourself, am I kind? Not just when it is beneficial to be kind, but even when it is not beneficial to be kind! That is what makes all the difference. The true Christian is kind in aspects of their life.

Goodness

Now what does Paul mean by goodness? Goodness does seem a bit general, but in this case, goodness refers to morals. Being honest in your morals and good in what you do on a day to day basis. A Christian who walks in the spirit does not waver in his moral depending in his or her situation. A good Christian is firm and unwavering in their morals no matter the situation!

Faithfulness

Faithfulness means that we walk by faith in everything we do. As we go about our lives, we leave everything in the hands of God knowing that he will do what is best for us. To be faithful means we are free of the anxiety and worry of life, knowing that God who takes care of the birds of the air will take care of us also. We have faith also that God is watching over us and hearing us!

Chapter Sixteen

Gentleness

To be gentle is an aspect of true Christianity. Think about it, if we are filled with love, faith, kindness and peace, chances are you are going to be quite gentle. Gentleness is not type of weakness and timidness. Gentleness is confidence in yourself as a person and God. So in all things you respond with gentle emotions as you have the peace of Christ within you.

Self-Control

Now finally the last of the fruits of the spirit is self-control. As we said earlier, the life of a Christian is about the struggle between the sinful desires of the flesh and the desire for true Life being through Christ. We as Christians need self-control, a life of fleshly indulgence is not compatible with a spiritual life!

Paul, thus completes his list of the Fruits of the Spirit and ends this chapter with the emphasise that we as Christians must crucify our flesh with its passion and desires so that we might truly be Christ-like!

If we live in the Spirit, let us also walk in the Spirit. Let us not become conceited, provoking one another, envying one another.

REFLECTION

Now that we've gone through each one, let's think about how we can strive to achieve the fruits of the spirit in our day to day lives. Remember that these are not unattainable characteristics of great saints, rather they are the results of a life with Christ that St. Paul endeavours all Christians to achieve. Let's hold ourselves to a high standard and strive Now that we've gone through each one, let's think about how we can strive to achieve the fruits of the spirit in our day to day lives. Remember that these are not unattainable characteristics of great saints, rather they are the results of a life with Christ that St. Paul endeavours all Christians to achieve. Let's hold ourselves to a high standard and strive always to walk in spirit!

If we live in the Spirit, let us also walk in the Spirit. Let us not become conceited, provoking one another, envying one another.

Chapter seventeen

We are now entering into the final chapter of St. Paul's epistle to the Galatians. What a journey it has been! Although Paul's epistle to the Galatians is relatively small, he has managed to say so much! And in this final chapter he concludes by leaving the Galatians with some spiritual advice and finally a blessing. Let's continue.

Generosity and Kinship

Now as Paul begins the final chapter of his epistle, he begins, in verse 1, by explaining how we should treat someone who is overtaken or struggling with sin. He states that if you have a member of the church who is sinning, be sure that someone who is spiritual among you support and restore him. Now this is some great advice for us today. As members of the church, it is on us to make sure than our fellow Christians are not living in sin, now how do we go about that? Paul is saying that someone who is spiritual should approach the person who is struggling and help them! Sometimes we prefer to judge the person and put them down, or even use a more aggressive means, however, this is not what St. Paul is encouraging. He actually states that we ourselves have to be careful to consider ourselves lest we also fall into sin when correcting them.

Paul then encourages the Galatians to bear one another burdens which in turn fulfills the law of Christ. This means that Christ, when instituting the church for us, wanted us to live with each other in a selfless and loving manner. That we support one another and help each other. You most likely go to church, when you go to church, do you have the willingness to help everyone in that church? Because that is what Christ is expecting of us, and that is what Christ wanted when He gave us the church. Of course, this needs to be done in humility, as Paul then continues and says:

"For if anyone thinks himself to be something, when is nothing, he deceives himself."

We need to be sure that as members of a church and the Body of Christ, we do not attribute any great deeds to ourselves, but rather we walk in humility, always telling ourselves that our good deeds are because of God's grace.

Now in the following verses it might sound like Paul is contradicting himself, let's have a read:

"But let each one examine his own work, and then he will have rejoicing in himself alone, and not in another. 5 For each one shall bear his own load."

What the Fathers Say

One who is spiritual yet has no compassion for his neighbour is his own deceiver, not knowing that the spirit of the law adds up finally to loving one another.
– St. Jerome

Repair your Brethren

The word Paul uses in the original Greek for restore is καταρτίζετε, this means to mend, repair or make complete again. This is a great reminder that when someone is sinning, we don't punish them or deal with them as if they have committed a crime, rather we should consider them as someone who is need of mending and thus, we help them to be repaired back to their original state which is the desire to live without sin and with Christ, of course!

People, Places &Things

> **What the Fathers Say**
>
> When someone steals another's clothes, we call them a thief. Should we not give the same name to one who could clothe the naked and does not? The bread in your cupboard belongs to the hungry; the coat unused in your closet belongs to the one who needs it; the shoes rotting in your closet belong to the one who has no shoes; the money which you hoard up belongs to the poor.
> – St. Basil the Great

But didn't Paul just say in the previous verse that everyone shall bear each other's load? Why is he now saying "each one shall bear his own load." Is Paul contradicting himself? Actually, there are a few explanations for this. The first being that both statements are working together, yes, we must support each other and always help on another and yes, we must also make sure that we are accountable for our own actions and deeds and not an unnecessary burden on others. For if everyone in the church allowed themselves to just throw all their problems on everyone around them, the church would not last very long, would it? Another perspective: Church Fathers state that Paul is referring to the Lord's judgment in verse 5. Meaning that everyman needs to understand that only you can bear the weight of your own sins, so don't expect anyone to carry your accountability for sin!

Finally, Paul's last piece of advice for a successful church is that anyone who is taught the Word of God should be sure to share good things with his teacher. For we are blessed when someone teaches us the ways or spiritually and reading the Bible. So in return, we must give to those who teach us. What does this look like today? Well today, we are blessed with priests and ministers who teach us and give up their time for us. It's important that we give back to them by, listening to what they say of course, but also supporting them financially through our church donations, for example. Remember that the church relies on all of us to chip in and do our part in order to function, so do not forget to pay blessings to those who teach you. Whether they are material blessings or a kind word.

To summarise Paul's advice for the church, lets put it into a list:

1. If someone at church is sinning, someone who is spiritual should gently help them
2. Help each other always, and bear the problems and burdens of one another
3. Remain humble and do not boast in your works
4. Hold yourself and only yourself accountable for your problems and sins
5. Repay and do good to those who teach the Bible

How beautiful are the words of Christ here!? Never forget that when we help those who are unfortunate, when we help those who are the least of us we are helping Christ.

Sheep and Goats?

You might be wondering why sheep and why goats in the parable we just looked at. Well, from an agricultural perspective, sheep were considered obedience, simple and peaceful. While goats were regularly stubborn and independent with a tendency to wander off. During the day, farmers would also allow the sheep and goats to graze the fields together, however, come night time, they had to be separated due to their differences. This represents the final day of judgement in Christ's parable.

People, Places &Things

But one might ask, "what are my gifts? I don't know what I have?" Well, look at what Christ says here, he did not make message of great talents of riches. He spoke about having food and sharing your food. He spoke about lending your time to those who are lonely. He spoke about being available for those who need you. I can guarantee that you have all these things, so how can we say, "I don't have anything" or "I don't know what to give." Let's take a moment to reflect and ask ourselves the following questions:

Am I helping others around me?

Am I using the blessings God gave me for good?

Do I desire to help others and be there for others?

REFLECTION

Let's take a moment to reflect and ask ourselves the following questions: Am I helping others around me? Am I using the blessings God gave me for good? Do I desire to help others and be there for others? Let's try our best to help someone this week without expecting anything in return!

Chapter Eighteen

CHAPTER EIGHTEEN

Goodness and Glory

Continuing on to verse seven, Paul wraps up his advice to the church by explaining to us a very important perspective. He explains that God is not mocked and that whatever we sow we will also reap, what does this mean? Well, to put it simply, Paul is saying you get out what you put in. Now this applies to all aspects of our Christian life. If we are half-hearted in prayer we cannot reap the true benefits of prayer. If we are in and out of church without consistency and not engaged, we cannot reap the true benefits of prayer. I have spoken to many people who have explained to me things such as, "I pray but I don't receive a response," or "I attend the liturgy but I am so bored," often when I asked this people how engaged they are in their prayer or the liturgy, chances are they are not putting in a lot of effort. Prayer, church, the liturgy and our general spiritual life with God is all about the amount of effort we put in. God can only work through us to the extent that we allow him to. Remember, once again, that God is knocking on our doors and He cannot come in unless we open to Him.

This is quite reminiscent of another Bible verse. In the Gospel of Matthew, Christ says the following:

Ask, and it will be given to you; seek, and you will find; knock, and it will be opened to you.
(Matthew 7:7)

We often remember the first part of that verse, but forget the rest. But what Christ is saying here is that you cannot simply get up once and ask God of something and expect

Chapter Eighteen

him to give it to you instantly. Prayer and spiritual life is a process. What does Christ say to do? Lets break it down into steps:

1. Ask – Of course you must genuinely ask God. Although God knows all that you want, you must humble yourself to stand and ask Him in prayer

2. Seek – Once you have asked, you must know seek the response and seek God's answer. How can we seek? By reading his Bible, by opening ourselves up to a relationship with him! By listening out for his word. You cannot hear God if you do not seek him

3. Knock – Finally, you must also take physical action. Knocking requires you to go to Church and physically act like a Christian. You cannot expect of God to give you everything you desire when you don't act Christ-like and you are not physically involved in a life with Him

What the Fathers Say

If the soul is vigilant and withdraws from all distraction and abandons its own will, then the spirit of God invades it and it can conceive because it is free to do so.
– St. Theophan the Recluse

Sowing and reaping

What does it actually mean to sow and to reap, and why are these terms so common place in the Bible? You might remember these terms from plenty of the parables of Christ. To sow refers to the planting of a seeds, just as a farmer must go out and plant seeds in his fields. To reap means to gather the crops that have sprouted as a result of your sowing. Now if you have sowed bad seeds, then you will of course, reap bad crops. The reason this analogy is so commonplace in the Bible is due to the fact that farming was apart of almost everyone's everyday life. And so, Christ and St. Paul give examples that are relevant to the people.

Paul now explains very clearly what happens to us if we sow according to the flesh. Meaning a life in which we give our flesh everything it wants and seek bodily desires. Of course, this can only lead to corruption and death. However, if we are focusing on our spirit and the will of the Spirit, we will reap heaven and eternity with our Creator. Paul continues, explaining to us to never weary from doing good, knowing that eventually we will reap great things. These great things are, once again, eternity.

As we go through out lives and we struggle with doing good, fasting, prayer and liturgy, remember always why you're doing all this. For you are doing the will of the Spirit so that you can one day achieve eternity!

Finally, Paul concludes this section by explaining to us to do good to all and especially those who are Christians and part of our faith!

> ## What the Fathers Say
>
> You must flee from sensual things. Indeed, every time a man comes near to a struggle with sensuality, he is like a man standing on the edge of a very deep lake and the enemy easily throws him in whenever he likes. But if he lives far away from sensual things, he is like a man standing at a distance from the lake, so that even if the enemy draws him in order to throw him to the bottom, God sends him help at the very moment he is drawing him away and doing violence.
> – Abba Poeman

Chapter Eighteen

> **What the Fathers Say**
>
> Prayer is being attached to God in all moments and situations of life. Then life becomes one prayer, without interruption or disturbance.
> —St. Basil the Great

Reflection

Sometimes being Christian is hard. Sometimes the last thing we want to do is pray, go to church or fast. It's okay to struggle with being Christian. But never forgot the true purpose of everything you are doing. I remember reading a book in which a character wanted to be a monk. His reason for being a monk was that, "If I believe that Christianity is the truth and heaven exists, how can I not dedicate every moment of my life to that truth?" I always found that such a compelling and very relevant to our lives today. If you truly believe that Christianity is the truth, then it is our duty to live everyday with our salvation in mind. It is our duty to ensure that we take the narrow path that leads to Life! So today, why don't we try our best to remember God in everything we do? Why don't we try and see God's goodness in everything and constantly remind ourselves of His heavenly kingdom that we are awaiting.

Chapter nineteen

CHAPTER NINETEEN

The Cross of Glory

Going back to St. Paul's people skills, he reveals to the Galatians how much he cares about them and the issues that they are facing by exclaiming that he has written this letter with his own hands! This tells the Galatians, that not only are these directly Paul's own words, but he was so moved by their situation that he could only trust himself to physically write this letter! This of course, emphasises to the Galatians his personal investment in their issues.

Now in the following verses, Paul reminds the Galatians to once again steer clear of the Judaizers. Let's have a look at what he says:

As many as desire to make a good showing in the flesh, these would compel you to be circumcised, only that they may not suffer persecution for the cross of Christ. 13 For not even those who are circumcised keep the law, but they desire to have you circumcised that they may boast in your flesh."

This is his final commentary on the Judaizers, just be he ends his letter. The emphasis of this statement is that the Galatians do not listen to those who focus on showing off their flesh or those who focus on things pertaining to the body! For these people are not willing to bear persecution for Christ anyway. Additionally, they focus on things such as circumcision, but they do not keep the law in other things. Paul emphasises that the only reason the Judaizers were so focused on the Galatians abiding by circumcision is so that they can boast and declare that they have influenced the Galatians to do such a thing.

This point is contrasted beautifully with verse 14, as Paul reminds us what the true source of our boasting should be:

> "But God forbid that I should boast except in the cross of our Lord Jesus Christ, by whom the world has been crucified to me, and I to the world."

How beautiful are the words of this great saint! We must always remind ourselves that our true source of joy and happiness, our true boast in all things in life is of course Christ and the salvation that He has granted us through his death on the cross. And by His death, the world no longer matters to us and we no longer matter to the world, for we have now transcended the fleshly body and have been permitted to access the divine state of unity with our beloved Christ! This emphasised further in Paul's emphasis of the fact that through Jesus, circumcision nor

What the Fathers Say

The Cross, is wood which lifts us up and makes us great ... The Cross uprooted us from the depths of evil and elevated us to the summit of virtue.
– St. John Chrysostom

People, Places & Things

Why is it important or even noteworthy that Paul is writing this letter with his own hands? Well back in those times, most letters were written by a scribe who was dictated what to write by the author. Most of Paul's letters were in fact written by someone else, while Paul dictated to the scribe what to write. This does not mean that Paul is not the author of those letters, rather he just did not physically write the letters himself, however they are his words. This method of writing letters was quite popular for people in positions in which they were regularly sending out multiple letters in a day. You can imagine that it would be quite difficult to write all your letters in a day with your own hands, thus the help of a scribe was greatly appreciated! Some scholars believe that St Luke was actually one of the scribes who helped St. Paul write a few of his letters!

> **What the Fathers Say**
>
> For wondrous indeed it was, that one who was blind from his birth should receive sight in Siloam, but what is this compared with the blindness of the whole world?... The glory of the cross led those who were blind through ignorance into light, loosed all who were held fast by sin, and ransomed the whole world of mankind
> – St. Cyril of Jerusalem

uncircumcision means anything, but what's important now is that we have received a new creation and that is salvation and the resurrection of the body!

Good Friday

During Good Friday in the Coptic Church, the church introduces the 6th hour prayers by opening with a Pauline epistle. The epistle chosen by the Fathers happens to be Galatians 6:14-18, beginning with Paul's famous words, But God forbid that I should boast except in the cross. The 6th hour being the time in which Christ was crucified, it is benefitting then that the church reminds us that our only boast should be in the cross of Christ that granted us salvation. What a beautiful contrast! The epistle is also read in a melancholic yet powerful ancient chant that sets the mood nicely for us to contemplate the Lord's crucifixion.

Chapter Nineteen

Reflection

Sometimes we forget how much Christ loves us. Sometimes, we are so focused on the troubles and anxieties of the world that we forget the bigger picture. We must learn to never forget what Christ done for us on the cross! And remind ourselves always, that if Christ, being God and the creator of this whole universe, died on the cross for me, how much more so will He take care of me in my day to day life! Everything will be okay because Christ, who died for us, is with us and will forever be with us. Let's remind ourselves today that God is in control, and He loves me.

Chapter twenty

The Final Blessing

At last, the final three verses of St. Paul's epistle to the Galatians leave us a with a blessing and few spiritual words.

Paul begins by calling the faithful followers of Christ the Israel of God. This is a reminder that we who are Christian are now the new Israel, not because of our ethnicity, or law, but because we follow the commandments of Christ in hopes of His salvation which He has made available for all!

Paul then requests of the Galatians that they no longer trouble him, for he bears the marks of the Lord Jesus. What does this mean, however?

The message here is that, Paul has suffered for his preaching of the gospel and not only has he experienced the suffering of Christ, but he is not a hypocrite and believes in what he is saying, so much so, that he is willing to suffer and die for his message. This, of course, is not something that the Judaizers are willing to do, for they boast only in the flesh. Now the marks of the Lord Jesus can refer to the scars of the flogging he has received multiple times and can also refer to the physical suffering of Christ, generally. Paul outlines, in detail, the physical torment he has received in 2 Corinthians, chapter 11. Once again, he is not showing the Galatians how tough he is, rather he is emphasising the credibility of his writing, since he has suffered immensely for it.

Finally, St. Paul ends with a blessing. Referring to the Galatians as fellow brethren and that the grace of Jesus may be with their spirits.

After a few years and a few more letters, the Apostle Paul finds himself imprisoned for a second time in Rome. Following one last letter to Timothy (2 Timothy), Paul is beheaded and dies for his faith in Christ and his preaching of the Gospel.

May the prayers of this great saint and martyr continually be with us all!

What the Fathers Say

The knowledge of the Cross is concealed in the sufferings of the Cross.
- St. Gregory the Great

REFLECTION

For our last reflection, I want you to think about your purpose in life. Just as St. Paul lived for Christ and the spreading of the Gospel, consider what type of life you want and how you would glorify God. For we as Christians are called to be a light to the world! Let's think about how we can do that in our life today and how we can serve God in everything we do.

www.ingramcontent.com/pod-product-compliance
Lightning Source LLC
Chambersburg PA
CBHW032300150426
43195CB00008BA/524